Marketing Dentistry Kaizen Style:

Small Steps to Big Profits

by

Dr. Bryan McLelland, DDS, BSc

First Printing, 2011

Printed in the United States of America

Disclaimer

This document contains business strategies, marketing methods, and other business advice that, regardless of my own results and experience, may not produce the same results (or any results) for you. I make absolutely no guarantee, expressed or implied, that by following the advice below you will make any money or improve current profits, as there are several factors and variables that come into play regarding any given business.

Primarily, results will depend on the nature of the product or business model, the conditions of the marketplace, the experience of the individual, and situations and elements that are beyond your control.

As with any business endeavor, you assume all risk related to investment and money based on your own discretion and at your own potential expense.

By reading this book, you assume all risks associated with using the advice contained within, with a full understanding that you, solely, are responsible for anything that may occur as a result of putting this information into action in any way, and regardless of your interpretation of the advice.

You further agree that the author cannot be held responsible in any way for the success or failure of your business as a result of the information presented below. It is your responsibility to conduct your own due diligence regarding the safe and successful operation of your business, if you intend to apply any of this information in any way to your business operations.

This book is dedicated to the three women in my life: my two daughters and wife who are blessings from above. They make the seemingly meaning-less so meaningful. Thank you.

Table of Contents

Introduction

This book has been created out of a passion for dentistry as a career and profession, and as a culmination of years of training, education, and experience that have come together to help and benefit dentists worldwide. Dentistry is an extremely rewarding profession when done with a heart full of service and love.

One of the greatest challenges dentists have when running a practice is the business side of dentistry. Secretly all dentists wish they could have all the benefits of a private practice without the burden of the business side of dentistry. This attitude comes from lack of training and experience running a small (and sometimes not so small) business. Business skills are acquired on the job for most dentists and healthcare professionals. Consequently, many mistakes are made on the road to success often leading to frustration.

The goal of this field guide is to help every dentist learn the essential skills of marketing their practice in a manner that is filled with action points. Large problems and large tasks can be overwhelming and marketing a dental practice well is definitely a large task. Kaizen is the perfect way to take on such a daunting task. At its core, Kai-zen represents a methodology of taking big tasks and breaking them down into smaller and small-er components until each individual component is no longer intimidating. These smaller compo-nents can then be mastered or completed and the sum total of all the small parts will equal an un-derstanding and mastery of the subject at hand.

It takes about 10,000 hours to master a subject and make you an expert in any given field. This breaks down to about five years of study to be-come an expert. In dentistry, it is my hope to help you become competent and effective in the area of marketing your practice since this will al-low you to reach the most people and do what you love...practice dentistry and serve your community.

To maximize your talents, get in the zone, and excel with the gifts we have been given honors our creator and our fellow man in the best way imaginable. In many ways, this is one of the most important goals in life. In that context, my purpose in writing this field guide is to help you attain this goal, giving more meaning and more purpose to your days practicing dentistry.

What is Kaizen?

The History of Kaizen

During World War II, Dr. Ed Demming, a statistician, was charged with increasing industrial output in the United States. Since it was wartime, innovative changes requiring major factory shut downs or overhauls were not financially feasible. Dr. Demming, therefore, introduced the concept of making small, sometimes seemingly insignificant changes. His concept resulted in dramatically increasing the manufacturing output of the United States and was a major reason the Allies won the war. After the war, Dr. Demming was forgotten in the United States but Japan recruited him to assist that country in its rebuilding effort. The Japanese perfected Dr. Demming's techniques and became an economic powerhouse. Decades later, America rediscovered Dr. Demming's old concepts, now adorned with a fancy new name...KAIZEN!

What is Kaizen?

Key elements of Kaizen include thinking small thoughts, asking small questions, taking small actions, solving small problems, bestowing small rewards, and identifying small moments.

Using Kaizen

This book examines using Kaizen to grow and market your dental practice by asking small questions, identifying small problems, and taking small action steps in order to solve small problems within your dental practice. Along the way, we will discuss reasons and ways to reward your team in small ways by identifying small moments of success.

Think of this book as a field guide for growth in marketing your practice. It may take you a month, six months, or a year or more to fully implement all the elements in this field guide. Enjoy the journey and be prepared for challenges. When obstacles occur, break them down into smaller elements, conquer each element, and move beyond the challenge. Life is a challenge. We should expect those challenges and look forward to overcoming them and growing in the process. The challenges in our life do not define us, but how we handle those challenges does. In the same way, the challenges we all have within our practices do not define our practices, but the way we handle those challenges does define our practice culture and ultimately who we are.

Getting Started

The first small step to take is to set aside time in your daily practice schedule for implementation and planning. This field guide contains many ideas and things to address in your practice. Acquiring new knowledge is of no value unless it is implemented and changes are made. This takes commitment and discipline. Right now call or email your scheduling team member and ask them to block out 30 minutes *immediately* after lunch two times per week. One time should be scheduled at the beginning of the week and the other time at the end of the week. If this seems like too much time, start with once a week. Do not schedule this time at the beginning of the day or it will be used for a coffee run or sleeping in. Do not schedule this time at the end of the day because you will not have the energy left this project deserves. Do not schedule this time just before lunch because this will get sucked up into patient care time when the morning runs over into the afternoon. Schedule this time immediately after lunch. Do it. Do it now!

Kaizen Action Plan/Checklist

☐ Schedule two weekly 30-minute planning sessions immediately after lunch.

☐ Include a key team member that knows how to get things done and isn't afraid of change.

Providing Cutting Edge Service in Dentistry

Cutting Edge Service

Delivering cutting edge service depends more on old fashion virtues such as caring and common sense, then it does following the latest trends or fads. It illustrates the marketing power of doing the little things that other practices neglect to do. Know that every team member performing a service is a marketer; from the dentist, to the hygienist, to the dental assistants, to the front desk team, to the janitor.

Innovation vs. Kaizen

Adopting every innovation or "big idea" in your practice only creates a temporary advantage that can not be sustained because other practices will inevitably copy the same innovations. Superior service is vital to sustaining the success initiated by any innovation or "big idea."

Sustaining high quality service requires:

1) Inspired leadership. In a dental practice, the dentist or perhaps an office manager needs to perform and fulfill the leadership roll. Know that leadership is a learned skill and can be acquired.

2) A patient-centered culture. Your dental practice should operate with systematically designed exceptional service, as well as effectively use information and technology.

Superior service is different in each practice and defines the personality or culture of your practice and makes it unique. Superior service is the sum total of the patient experience within your practice. Patients will decide if your service was negative, neutral, or positive based on many small points of contact. Improving these small points of contact is at the heart of Kaizen.

The Product

The product the patient is buying is the dental service or performance. Another way of saying this is that the patient is buying and paying for an experience --- rather than simply a crown, bridge restoration, filling, cleaning, etc. The patient is paying for you and your dental team and will continue to patronize your practice because of your practice culture. This is quite different from a business that sells items or goods.

Goods vs. Services

Goods are generally first produced and then sold, whereas services are sold before they are produced. For example, a Sonicare® toothbrush is made before the patient purchases the product (the Sonicare® toothbrush). However, in the case of a full mouth reconstruction, the service is paid for before it (full mouth reconstruction) is produced and the full value is appreciated. This relationship create difficulties but also opportunities for dentists. We must first recognize and fully appreciate what it means to offer a service and be in the service industry.

Services are Intangible

Dentistry is an intangible, meaning the patient must experience it to really know it. This intangibility makes dentistry more difficult for customers to imagine and desire than goods and items. Consequently, word-of-mouth marketing has a prominent effect in winning patients' loyalty and hearts. Word-of-mouth marketing creates a network of friends and family. This network of people appreciates your practice culture and they are willing to pay you to experience that culture. Network marketing is built on this incredibly powerful principle.

Returning Patients

Whether or not patients return to your practice will be strongly influenced by your dental team and personnel. How your team acts, what they say, what they do not say, and their overall appearance are all factors that will influence a patient's decision to return to your practice or refer others to it.

For example, your front desk team member is likely to be the first person a new patient will speak with on the phone, the first person the patient will see when they walk through the front door, and the last person the patient will see as they exit your practice on the date of service. The significance of this can not be underestimated and the position can not be filled by someone that is anything less than exceptional.

Many dentists find themselves with an employee in this position who has been promoted beyond his or her skill set because he or she is a long time employee. Typically this person is merely acceptable or barely acceptable at this position.

The first small Kaizen step is to use your scheduled time just after lunch to write out the necessary or desired traits and skills for each key position in your office. Typical positions in a dental practice include front desk, financial coordinator, dental assistant, dental hygienist, and dentist. For each position, write down two columns: one for personality traits and one for skills.

After listing personality traits and skills for each position, decide which of these are absolutely mandatory and which are simply desirable. You may also choose to ask your team members to assist you in creating these lists in a staff meeting.

Your completed lists next need to be utilized for two purposes:

1)   When hiring people in the future, these lists need to be at the top of your mind when selecting a new team member. Use these lists and do NOT compromise.

2)   Examine each position in your practice and determine whether your current employee has all the mandatory skills you have listed for each position.

One well-known practice management consultant estimates the cost of training each new employee at well over $30,000. The cost of a team member that will never obtain the traits you have listed as important to his or her position is massive and should not be tolerated. If you find you have a team member in the wrong position, make a plan to move them into a position in your practice where they can shine. If you do not have a position in your practice that meets your employee's skill set, you must allow them to leave your employ and move on to a place where he or she will have the opportunity to shine.

Every practice needs to have the right people on the bus and the right people in the correct seats on the bus. To keep someone in a position of incompetence is not fair to either your practice or your employee. Give your employee a chance to find a place where he or she can shine. Do not hold your employees back.

Next create a list of traits and skills that you would desire in a future dental associate. Compare the list you create to your own traits and skills. If your lists do not match, do not fire yourself. Decide which of the skills you desire are trainable or attainable and which are not. You will need to hire someone with the skills you do not possess if they are mandatory and compensate for this deficiency.

Even if you do not possess a specific skill but believe it to be attainable, you should ask yourself whether that task is the best use of your time. Bookkeeping is a great example of a skill that you may have listed and could be learned, but it is also easily delegated and, as the dentist, you should spend as much time as possible performing dentistry for your practice's greatest profitability.

Once you have completed your employee analysis, pat yourself on the back and reward yourself and your employees with a small treat such as ice cream.

Service Marketers - Dentists

Dentists must be effective with new and existing patients, and internal customers. Internal customers are your team. They are often forgotten in the equation, but since your practice's service is evaluated by the performance your entire team delivers, they are very important to the patient's experience.

Getting it Right the First Time

Service reliability means performing dentistry dependably and accurately. When dentistry is delivered carelessly, avoidable mistakes are made in the delivery, or promises are not kept and the patient's confidence is shaken.

From the patient's perspective, proof of a great dentist is in flawless delivery. Perfect crown margins, great selection of dental materials, and flawless anatomy in restorative dentistry are examples of things that are important to dentists but imperceptible to the patient. We all know dentists with terrible technical dentistry skills who have very successful practices. The secret of their success lies in patient perceptions of the practice's service.

While technical skills are important, for our purposes we assume you have these skills and that you want the opportunity to share them with as many patients as possible. To consistently grow your practice, providing flawless service is paramount.

The Tangibles

"Usually" is not good enough ---- especially when you view things from your patients' perspectives. When service delivery fails for a patient, your practice has failed 100% of the time for that patient. When the injection of local anesthetic makes a patient unexpectedly numb, the fact that this happens very rarely is of little comfort to that patient. You may have a 95% success rate in service deliverance, but it is important to remember that, from the perspective of the remaining 5%, your failure to deliver service is absolute and 100%.

Reliability is the most important factor, but it is not the only factor. Tangibles, responsiveness, assurance, and empathy are also important.

Tangibles are the appearance of the clinic, the equipment, the staff members, and communication materials such as brochures, health history forms, and paperwork. This brings us to your next task which is to address each of these tangibles.

Clinic Appearance

First, look at your clinic. Go outside and walk up to the building as a patient would. Take a note pad and pen and be critical. Write down what you like and what you do not like. Walk into the waiting room, sit down, and write down more thoughts. Then go to the radiology area. Follow your normal patient flow and notice what everything looks like, feels like, and smells like in every location. Note the emotions your tour invokes in you. You may also choose to assign other team members to go through the same process and submit their insights to you.

The next step is to evaluate all of your own comments and those of your team's. Make a list of areas needing improvement. Then, place a star beside the things that can be changed easily and cost effectively. Delegate a team member to get those things changed ASAP.

Once those improvements have been made, purchase pastries for your office as a small reward for successfully completing this step.

In completing the physical evaluation of your office, you have noticed small things, taken small actions, and bestowed small rewards...making Dr. Demming proud!

Return to your list of needed improvements and examine the remaining items --- those that could not be changed relatively easily or inexpensively. Evaluate the remaining items, approximating cost in terms of both time and money needed to make those changes. Then number the remaining items in terms of priority. Tackle those items that have high priority and relatively low cost. Reward your team again.

The items left are the time consuming and expensive items that will take some planning. Group and prioritize these items and take the following two steps:

1) Create a step-by-step, clearly defined plan for completion of each project, including obtaining bids when necessary; and

2) Create a savings plan to get the job(s) done. Set up an automatic, bi-weekly transfer of funds from your business checking account to a special account dedicated to this purpose. The amount of funds transferred need only be a nominal and reasonable amount. You can use Kaizen to set up small transfers and slowly increase the amount, keeping the

level comfortable until you have the capital required to complete the project(s).

When the necessary funds are available in your special account for each project, it is just a matter of setting the time and activating the plan. Good job for getting this done. Reward yourself with a nice dinner out on the town with someone special. Tell your dinner guest about your success and the small steps you have taken to accomplish those steps using Kaizen. Teaching a subject to someone helps to cement and solidify the learning process for the teacher, taking your knowledge level to new heights.

Office Staff

Walk through your clinic to take a critical look at your staff. Are they dressed appropriately? Are they groomed well? Based on their appearance, do they look like people you would want taking care of your mom?

Disney© has strict grooming and dress codes for their "cast members" and so should every dental office. Your dress code needs to be enforced. Assign one of your team members who passed your first evaluation to the small task of monitoring the dress code in your practice. Teach your dress code monitor that he or she should gently remind team members about the dress code when they do not adhere to it. If necessary, your monitor should inform you of continual breaches in your grooming and dress code.

Consider whether you have provided your staff with clear instructions regarding your dress code, as well as any tools and resources necessary to meet the code, such as uniforms. A small clothing allowance given to each team member could assist in your staff's cooperation with the dress code. Another Kaizen approach would be to reward your team with lunch after three weeks of maintaining perfect dress code and grooming habits. This will allow for the formation of a new habit that will naturally become a part of the culture of your practice.

Paperwork

Now take your paperwork and evaluate the look and feel of it. Does it represent the quality and character of your practice? Does it need updating? There are many cost effective ways to engage a person to give you a makeover in this department. If it has been five or more years since you have had an outsider look at this for you, then you are due for an update.

Responsiveness

Responsiveness is defined as the willingness to provide prompt service. You need to empower your team to solve problems and to make decisions in order to have maximum responsiveness.

Allow team members to invest a small amount of money in solving a patient problem. Set this amount at a level you are comfortable with. Give your team members the ability to take small risks and make small decisions to help out patients and be responsive.

Beware of pitfalls in your practice that can prevent this culture from developing. For example, team members will stop solving problems and responding to patient issues the instant they are undermined or reprimanded by doctors or office managers, particularly when done in public. Allow your team to make mistakes and learn and grow from those mistakes. When mistakes occur, and we all know they will occur, teach the entire team about those mistakes in a non-threatening way that does not point out the individual responsible for the mistake.

Assurance

Assurance refers to the knowledge and the courtesy of the dental team and their ability to convey trust and confidence. In short, assurance is the ability of your team to make your patient feel comfortable and full of trust in your practice and the doctor.

Empathy

Empathy means providing caring and individualized attention to patients, which is especially important in dentistry and in all health care fields for obvious reasons. Empathic listening lets your patients know that you hear them and care about their problems/issues. Once the patient knows that you care, trust is built. A patient will not accept solutions to dental problems until they know you understand their issues/problems and care about how they are feeling. Why would anyone accept a solution from someone who they think does not understand their problem? If this disconnect exists, it shows a lack of understanding and trust and will hamper patient acceptance.

Benefits of Reliable Service

Profits are maximized when dentistry is performed well and right the first time. Providing reliable service improves marketing effectiveness, improves operating efficiency, and increases patient retention rates.

High patient retention rates are important because they decrease the need to obtain new patients. More dentistry can be performed on a per patient basis from current patients, which also increases word-of-mouth communication/ referrals and network building. Outside patient referrals and new patient exams organically increase your profitability and revenue generated per hour.

When an error in service occurs and a task needs to be re-done, not only is there a cost in performing the task again, but there is also lost opportunity. The chair time spent taking another impression for a crown preparation could have been spent restoring an implant. Getting the job done correctly the first time should always be the goal.

Striving for 100% Service Reliability

Striving for 100% service reliability is worth the effort. Not only will it increase your profits, it will also lead to a positive work environment that engenders high productivity and low cost by enhancing employee morale, enthusiasm, and commitment.

Delivering a Reliable Service

The criteria defining flawless service are more subjective than concrete. A patient's expectations and requirements are the only real standards and measuring stick for reliability. This may have very little to do with the quality of dentistry and a lot to do with performing or delivering it in a way that appears flawless.

Effectively tackling these challenges requires leadership, thorough testing and retesting of dental services, and building a culture of error-free service.

Leadership

Building a reliable service practice requires strong leaders with a passion for perfection. These strong leaders (dentists and office managers) are the life blood of a reliability-centered service strategy. Dentists are naturally perfectionists and well suited for this task. Leaders must firmly believe that 100% reliability is feasible. They must frequently and effectively communicate that belief to their teams and actively reward error-free service in small ways. Strong leaders are never content with the status quo and strive for continuous improvement. They choose to foster an attitude that says: "If it is not fixed, it will break." rather than "If it ain't broke, don't fix it." In this manner, your dental practice will be thoroughly tested.

If you are a dentist and not a strong leader, then you need to work on leadership skills and/or hire a strong office manager with these leadership skills. Hiring a strong office manager is better than having no leadership in a practice, but it takes a distant second to the doctor taking the leadership role in a practice.

Leadership is a learned behavior and can be taught. Take small Kaizen steps, read books on leadership, take classes on leadership, and pick targeted areas to improve leadership skills. Use your 30 minute time slots to read books on leadership and educate yourself. The internet is full of educational sources on this topic.

You may choose to start with privately developing a vision and mission statement. Take this to a staff meeting and modify the vision and mission statement based on team discussions.

Use the time set aside to create one-, three-, and five-year plans. Mark your calendar to revisit your plans and update them yearly. Small Kaizen actions, such as simply writing your plans down, will substantially increase the likelihood that you will succeed in those plans. Writing your plans down is a psychokinetic action that imprints the subconscious mind and drastically increases the likelihood of completing the desired goals.

Service Testing

Dentists should create a service blueprint for their practices. A service blueprint depicts the service, service events, and processes in a flow chart. This document is useful for planning and diagnosis. It creates a tangible method for evaluating a service and its delivery.

Typically, practices leave services to individuals and their talents and then manage the pieces, rather than the whole. To do a thorough service testing of your practice, you need to create a blueprint on paper for each individual and process. This is Kaizen to the core. Dental practices should complete this process with financial, accounts payable, accounts receivable, new patient phone calls and visits, established patient phone calls and visits, consult visits and treatment visits, case presentations by the doctor, and financial presentations. Any routine process that happens with a patient encounter or in management of that encounter, as well as routine business processes, should be blueprinted in this way.

Work these processes out on paper and in flow charts, simplifying and trouble shooting with 100% reliability of service in mind. Before offering a new service, map out the blue print of that service in detail. Implementing electronic medical records, a NuCalm™ treatment, hybrid implant restorations, or advanced cosmetic dentistry should all be worked out and broken down into small steps (service blueprinting) prior to going live with those items. Creating service blueprints prior to providing the service will enhance its implementation and success.

NuCalm™

NuCalm™ is an innovative drug-free way of providing comfort and relaxation to patients. The system uses neuroacoustic software, cranial electrical stimulation (CES), L-Theanine and Gaba with blockout glasses to induce a near sleep state which is very relaxing. The advantages to a clinician are obvious and include decreased team and dentist anxiety and stress because the dentist and staff do not have to "feel" the stresss of their patients. Each of these components has been used individually, with success, on Post-Traumatic Stress Disorder patients for decades. A sample of a blueprint for implementation of this technology in a dental practice is included in Appendix A of this book.

Post-Launch Testing

Conduct research on your service on an ongoing basis. You can do this by using mystery patients and soliciting information from both patients and employees. Employees have an excellent vantage point. Create a reporting method or form that employees can fill out when a patient reports a problem. These forms need to be collected, organized, analyzed, and then acted on to be useful. Your 30 minute time slots can be used for this important activity.

Attitude

Your goal is to create systems designed for error free patient care. These systems all involve personnel and teamwork issues. The quality of the practice that your team experiences internally strongly influences the quality of service your team provides to your patients. It is important to understand how an employee's attitudes and behaviors can erode or enhance your service and reputation.

Once the goal of 100% service reliability is explained and outlined by the leaders in a practice, attitude is everything. Each team member should want, expect, and be willing and able to provide error free service. All team members must believe this an important and worthy goal. We all understand that error free service may not, in reality, be possible 100% of the time, but it is vital to strive for this and use teamwork and synergy toward achieving this goal. Targeting anything less will guarantee service errors and unhappy patients.

Teamwork

A lack of interdepartmental understanding, cooperation, and communication contributes significantly to unreliable service. For example, if the scheduling department does not understand the financial department's role in patient care, and the financial department does not understand the dental assistant's role, and the dental assistant does not understand scheduling issues, a toxic loop will create unreliable service and poor patient experiences. Sometimes patients will wonder if they are dealing with one unified practice. Not only will this type of experience frustrate patients, but it will also frustrate the entire team, adversely affecting performance. One team member should never blame another part of the practice for a service error.

Create a care pair who will walk the patient through his or her experience, integrating front staffing items with procedural or back staffing items. In addition, you may choose to assign one person to integrate services for all areas of the practice. Cross-training of team members so that each member understands the entire process is vital to creating an integrated practice.

Kaizen Action Plan/Checklist

☐ Does everyone in your practice believe that 100% reliability is a worthy goal? If not, why?

☐ Does everyone in your practice have a good grasp of the challenges involved in striving for 100% service reliability?

☐ Do you demonstrate your commitment to service reliability to all of your employees?

☐ Does your practice rigorously test new services prior to implementation?

☐ Does your practice continuously re-evaluate your services after introduction?

☐ Are you doing enough to ensure that your team is able, motivated, and encouraged to aim for zero service errors? Do you ensure your team does not feel undermined when they respond to patients' needs? Do you refrain from reprimanding employees in public?

☐ Hiring the right people for the right positions and then training them to recognize error free service delivery are the keys. Do you have the right people on the bus and in the right seats on the bus?

☐ Do you encourage teamwork and communication across functional units? Do you cross-train your employees? Create a time table to cross-train all team members in all positions.

Service Error Recovery

Getting it Very Right the Second Time

Despite zero service error attitudes and goals, stuff happens. Complaining patients are often viewed as the enemy or a source of irritation. This attitude is counterproductive. It is important to know that premeditated thefts of services by patients are quite rare. For example, in other industries, these occurrences are estimated at 1% to 2% of the time. Unfortunately, what can happen if we are not careful is that the 98% of our patients who are honest can be treated like criminals in order to try to catch the 1% to 2% who are true crooks. Give your patients the benefit of the doubt and assume the best in people.

Benefits of Strong Service Recovery

Patients pay more attention to a practice's performance when things go awry than when things run smoothly. Retreating services get scrutinized. These situations provide an opportunity for communicating commitment to your patients and strengthening their loyalty to your practice, but they must be handled correctly.

What do customers value in service performance? The following is a list of positive service attributes identified by customers.

Top 10 Service Attributes:

1) Being called back when promised.
2) Receiving an explanation of how a problem happened.
3) Being provided with information such as what number to call.
4) Being contacted promptly when a problem is resolved.
5) Being allowed to talk to someone in authority.
6) Being told how long it will take to solve a problem.
7) Being given useful alternatives if a problem cannot be solved.
8) Being treated like a person, not a number.
9) Being told about ways to prevent a future problem.
10) Being given a progress report if a problem cannot be resolved immediately.

This list of service attributes is actually from the banking industry --- not dentistry. However, numbers one, four through six, and eight and nine translate directly to dentistry. Six out of the 10 attributes listed pertain to problem resolution. Please understand that there is a direct monetary value to this.

When Service Problems Occur

A patient's confidence will be shaken, but not shattered unless the problem reinforces a recurring pattern of previous shortcomings or the recovery effort fails to satisfy the patient. Therefore, effective service recovery is not a cure for chronic unreliability.

Service Recovery Defined

Service recovery is an all out recovery effort when occasional but inevitable service snafus occur.

Guidelines

First, do not perceive these situations as unproductive, unprofitable, and unpleasant interruptions. They cannot be made low priority. An interesting and dangerous paradox exists. Practices with excellent service reliability are prone to mishandling service errors because they are not used to dealing with repercussions of delivering poor service. They may be ill-prepared and reluctant to handle problems effectively because they happen so infrequently.

Identify the Service Problems

The first step to problem resolution is to unravel the patient's disappointments. After the source(s) of their grievances have been identified, prompt internal and external actions must be taken. Internal actions resolve the problem. External actions include apologizing, acknowledging your awareness of your patient's dissatisfaction, and informing the patient that corrective measures are being taken.

Conduct Patient Research

Ask your patients for feedback about your practice. This shows caring and concern for service, but it must be genuine. Consider forming a patient focus group and invite key patients in to discuss issues with your practice. Team members should be attentive observers and see problems as they occur. They can then surprise patients by correcting service shortfalls "live." Also, employ the "mystery shopper" method by using mystery patients.

Monitor Service Problems

Anticipating problems requires behind-the-scenes monitoring of the general service process. To monitor, begin by scrutinizing a service blueprint. Identify possible fail points where a breakdown in services is at risk of occurring. During this step, keep in mind that when patients are transferred from one team member or function or area in the practice to another that this is a potential point of failure.

Failing to devise and implement a proactive recovery effort is often a more serious shortfall in the eyes of customers than the basic problem. People expect errors and mistakes to occur and are tolerant of those if they are handled appropriately.

Resolve Problems Efficiently

Resolving problems efficiently involves two factors: (1) your team members; and (2) your practice's ability to make amends for the hassle your patients feel.

Nurture the People Factor

Responsiveness, assurance, and empathy result from the human performance of your team. How your employees handle problem resolution largely determines the result for the patient. Results are either positive (satisfactory to the patient) or a double deviation (unsatisfactory) which can be catastrophic to your patient and practice. Therefore, it is especially important to have the right team member resolve a problem and to empower that employee adequately to do so.

Prepare your employees for service error recovery with proper training on how to bend the rules, improvise, and take charge. Empower employees to solve problems so that they are not hand cuffed with the lack of power to execute problem resolution. Consider setting a dollar amount that employees can use to solve problems on their own initiatives. This amount may be greater than the service actually generated before the service error occurred, but the extra cost will be money well spent to maintain patient satisfaction which is necessary to obtain repeat business and referrals.

Facilitate team members with technology and information to help resolve problems including up-to-date phone systems, practice management systems, and electronic medical records (EMR).

Psychological support, including stress management, is important for the team member(s) dealing with problem resolution since this is a tough task. Courses on stress management, group meetings with peers to discuss problems, and facilities for physical exercise may be useful to help manage this stress. Reward employees with small rewards such as lunch vouchers/gift cards and recognition. Have available a relatively large number of small awards to give to anyone who makes an all out recovery effort. Then give a few higher level rewards and publicize widely and loudly the specific accomplishments of higher levels of recovery as examples and inspiration. These small steps will help build a positive practice culture.

Make Amends for the Hassle Factor

Whenever a patient experiences a service problem, they are forced to sacrifice something. Gift cards from local coffee shops and restaurants can show your understanding of and help compensate for the inconvenience your patients have experienced.

Learn From the Recovery Experience

Learn to view service errors as an opportunity to learn how to get better. When service errors occur, conduct a root cause analysis to fix the source of the problem. Break the issue down into its core elements to identify the moment of breakdown and resolve this issue permanently.

Monitor Service Systems and Processes

An ongoing system that captures information pertaining to each instance of recovery service is mandatory for maximizing benefits that can result from recovery efforts. Your system can be created either manually or through software that is available for this purpose. Being aware of the service recovery efforts that are occurring allow the dentist/manager to look for patterns and areas of chronic weakness so that changes can be made to eliminate the service errors.

Kaizen Action Plan/Check List

☐ Does your practice have an effective system for capturing patient complaints?

☐ Does your practice make it easy to complain?

☐ Do you conduct formal research on service problems? Do you conduct online surveys (i.e. through websites such as Survey-Monkey™) or patient focus groups? Are your team members attentive observers?

☐ Do you systematically monitor potential fail points in your practice? Do you set aside time to create service blueprints? Do you periodically review your service blueprints for any necessary modifications?

☐ Are your team members prepared and encouraged to excel in resolving service problems?

☐ Is your practice sensitive to the hassle factor or patient inconvenience in getting service problems resolved?

☐ Do you strive to expose the root cause of service problems?

☐ Do you modify your service process monitoring based on recovery experiences? Are you alert to previously unnoticed fail points?

☐ Do you have an effective problem tracking
system? Is the information reviewed rou-
tinely?

Exceeding Expectations

Patients assess service quality by comparing what they expect with what they receive. Patients are the sole judge of service. When they judge service, they do so based on a scale that consists of their desired level of service at the top and what they consider to be an adequate level of service at the bottom of the range. Their zone of tolerance is between these two levels of service. Sometimes dentists fall into the trap of deciding for themselves when service is adequate. It is a dangerous practice to forget who the ultimate judge of adequate service is because it will inevitably lead to poor service.

Zone of Tolerance

The zone of tolerance can vary from patient to patient and even from interaction to interaction. Patients will evaluate the practice's reliability, tangibles, responsiveness, assurance, and empathy on this scale. The more important the area of service to the patient, the smaller the patient's zone of tolerance will be.

Reliability, or delivering the dentistry promised, is the most valued factor to patients. The remaining four factors will be judged based on how the dentistry is delivered.

Managing Expectations

Exceeding expectations earns intense patient loyalty and should therefore become a goal of your practice. In order to exceed patient expectations, you must first manage them. Managing expectations occurs through managing the promises made, dependably performing the dentistry promised, and effectively communicating with patients.

Manage Promises Made

Ensure that any promises made to patients reflect reality. Beware of both explicit and implicit promises. Over promising undermines the patient's tolerance and trust. If your practice under promises and over delivers, it will lead to greater patient satisfaction. Disappointment occurs when expectations are not matched with delivery. A patient's expectations may or may not be realistic. Creating or clarifying patient expectations can help a practice immensely. If you find that patients are consistently disappointed in a particular area in your practice, you know that their expectations are not being met. Step back and see what expectations patients have and where those expectations come from. It may be that *implicit* messages are creating expectations that are not being met. If that is the case, *explicit* clarification to the patient of what he or she can expect with any given interaction/appointment/procedure may immediately help your practice exceed or at least match the patient's expectations.

Place a Premium on Reliability

Reliability is foremost to patients. If your practice is reliable, the need for service recovery is limited or eliminated, which reduces stress and energy output for both your team and your patients. When errors occur, expectations go up because tolerance goes down and awareness increases. In other words, do it right the first time --- be reliable.

Communicate with Patients

Regular communication with your patients to understand their expectations and concerns, to explain the services they receive, and to express appreciation for choosing your practice builds good will and positive additions in their emotional bank accounts. This builds tolerance. Email presents an opportunity to communicate regularly and cost effectively with patients. Websites such as www.constantcontact.com and www.mailchimp.com can assist with e-mail updates. The website www.surveymonkey.com can create a survey e-mail campaign.

Exceeding Patient Expectations

Once you manage your expectations, you are then in a position to exceed them. This is done by excelling in service delivery. Treat patients with uncommon grace, courtesy, and caring. Alert team members can capitalize on opportunities that arise to troubleshoot, solve problems, and exceed expectations. Small moments like sending flowers to a patient's upcoming wedding that may have come up in conversation is an example of ways to exceed expectations.

Service recovery situations are golden opportunities for exceeding expectations. The patient's expectations are higher during recovery, but the opportunity to exceed is also greater. You must therefore be responsive, empathetic, and reassuring. This is imperative for success.

Establishing a Patient Franchise

A patient franchise is defined as unwavering patient loyalty. Exceptional service can intensify patient loyalty to the point they tune out competitive options. Periodic research to monitor patient expectations can drive the development of strategies for exceeding expectations.

Kaizen Action Plan/Check List

☐ Does your practice strive to present a realistic picture of your service to patients? Are you aware of both explicit and implicit expectations?

☐ Is performing the dentistry right the first time a top priority in your practice?

☐ Do you communicate effectively with patients? Do you ask them what they want and thank them for their business?

☐ Do you surprise patients during their visits with small pleasantries?

☐ Do your team members view service problems as opportunities or problems/annoyances?

☐ Do you continuously evaluate and improve your performance against patient expectations? Does your practice have a patient satisfaction survey that is automatically employed? Satisfaction surveys should be built into the normal practice routine. Consider help from websites like www.surveymonkey.com.

Build Your
Marketing Efforts

Marketing Director

The Marketing Director's role in your practice is to turn everyone else into clever marketers. The Marketing Director's goal should be to turn your practice into a marketing institution, rather than providing marketing services for the practice.

First, your Marketing Director should determine your practice's marketing message and then integrate marketing efforts into the business plan. A Marketing Director is a change architect who helps your practice by redefining and modifying strategic directions and responses to changes in the market. Marketing Directors also help renew practices by defining their strategic directions and internal measures necessary to achieve those goals. They capitalize on the reality that team members providing services to patients are in the best position to be marketers.

Marketing directors need to push, pull, and prod team members to want to be and know how to be effective marketers. Directors not only persuade patients to buy, but also team members to perform. Marketing Directors educate team members about marketing efforts. They need to make it easier for employees to market the practice. For example, patient information files can be created to help teams understand who their patients are and what their needs and goals are. Practice management systems that speed transactions and free employees for marketing assist in this effort. Internal training and cross-training to make team members more competent and confident is paramount.

A Marketing Director understands that the willingness and ability of team members to continuously engage in marketing behaviors are key marketing strategies. The director must be the leader and the champion of service quality. He or she must manage the image of the practice. Transforming similarity into distinctiveness is not easy when the products or differences lie in the performance which is typical in dentistry. Set aside time to decide who in your practice has the required skills and talents to be the Marketing Director. If you do not have the correct person in your practice, consider hiring someone for this position or making it a part of an existing position. Train the current person in this position on how to complete this dynamic process.

There are many dentists providing the same basic product. The differences among practices lie in their service or personality. The goal is to create a patient franchise --- undying patient loyalty that causes your patients to tune out the competition because they are smitten by your practice's culture.

A Marketing Director must know what these differences are and communicate them cohesively, consistently, and strikingly. As Jim Collins writes in *Good to Great*, you need to know what your "hedge hog" concept is. The Marketing Director must ask questions such as "What does your practice do well?" and "What is your reason for existence?" Every sensory stimulus communicates something about your practice. These need to be mobilized into one powerful message by your practice's Marketing Director and management.

The more complicated the dentistry you provide, the more important it is to create confidence in the people who are producing the service. Before and after photos of patients and patient testimonials can be very helpful. Credentials and training of team members is paramount. Remember that changing and modifying the practice culture can be painful and require one step back for every two steps forward.

Kaizen Action Plan/Check List

- ☐ Are you on the cutting edge of change in your practice? Are you on top of changing markets, technologies, competitors, and legislative/regulatory patterns for dentistry?
- ☐ Do you have a practice blueprint for what you wish to be? Do you have an action plan on how you will actually move the practice in the new direction? Is your action plan broken down into small steps in order to decrease fear and failure?
- ☐ Are you actively teaching marketing in your practice? Start small. Be consistent.
- ☐ What are you doing to facilitate marketing in your practice?
- ☐ Do you listen to your internal customers and team members?
- ☐ Do you know the obstacles to delivering exceptional service?
- ☐ Is your practice dealing with the branding opportunity comprehensively and strategically?
- ☐ Is your practice developing new services?
- ☐ Consider a practice promotion video and testimonial video to be shown daily in your office/waiting room, as well as posted on your website.

Maximizing
Your Practice

Managing the Evidence

The intangible nature of services in dentistry specifically has important implications for how patients form impressions and make buying decisions. Before making the purchase, they are attentive to tangible clues about the service. The question is: Will the patient experience the practice's intended or unintended evidence?

The tangible evidence your practice provides therefore needs to be designed to nurture and support the desired attitudes and impressions you want the patient to have. The tangible evidence includes your practice's physical environment, communication, and fees.

The Physical Features

Design features of your office including the architecture and the layout of both the interior and exterior of your practice can affect the evidence.

Ambient factors like air temperature and noise levels need to be controlled to avoid negative influences. Controlling unwanted or inappropriate conversation by team members is paramount. In most dental offices, sound carries and conversations are heard by patients when you least expect it. As a test, sit in your waiting room or a treatment room and listen to conversation from a patient's perspective. Sound control systems can be installed in your office in key locations to eliminate travel of voices at nominal costs and are worth their weight in gold. For more information about an effective sound control system, visit www.officeprivacy.com and read about The VoiceArrest™ Sound and Speech Privacy System.

The appearance of your team members will affect the patient's perceptions. Patients will equate sloppy, dirty looking employees with your service quality.

The appearance and behavior of other patients can also affect the patient's perceptions. For example, a waiting room full of postsurgical patients bruised, swollen, and moaning leaves a certain impression that will make elective cosmetic dentistry patients less likely to accept treatment.

Control your practice's tangible evidence by providing before and after books, patient testimonial books, educational videos, and practice promotion videos, which leave a distinctly different and positive impression.

Communications

Another form of evidence that patients will use to make judgments about your service are your communications. Billing statements, letterhead, advertising signage, newsletters, and word-of-mouth communication send clues about your service. Be sure your communications align with the message you want to send.

Excellent practices emphasize existing evidence or create new evidence. They can make their dentistry tangible by emphasizing the final results of the service. For example, a beautiful white smile and the increase in self-confidence a patient received by having the smile they always wanted are two end results that highlight the benefits of dental care. This creates a tangible representation of the service.

Make Your Message Tangible

Encourage word-of-mouth communication. This is especially important for dentistry because the consequences to patients of picking the wrong provider/practice are significant. Merge comments from existing patients into your advertising. Leave positive patient comments or testi-monial books in the waiting room. Create a brochure for your practice that is "from patients." You may also choose to guarantee your services to your patients because you send a message to potential patients that your service must be excellent. If it wasn't, you would not guarantee your service. It also sends a message to your dental team that your practice must provide excellent service because you are guaranteeing it. Use guarantees cautiously in dentistry.

Prices/Fees

Patients also view fees as a clue about the dentistry. Fees are a visible indicator of the service level and quality of the dentistry. When fees are too low, patients may wonder if the quality is poor. Patients may wonder if your practice's philosophy is: "You get what you pay for." On the other hand, when fees are too high, patients may think they are getting a "poor value" or rip-off. Setting fees not only determines profitability, but it also sends a message.

Rules of Evidence

When creating the tangible evidence, think of how you want your patients and employees to feel and respond. You need to manage and shape their first impressions. You need to manage the trust factor as well as facilitate quality service. If necessary, change your image and provide sensory stimulation to support this change in image.

Remember to socialize employees and educate them on providing appropriate evidence.

The phone skills of the receptionist are critical in determining the patient's first impressions. Scripting is a helpful way to manage conversations and control verbiage. Examining all routine patient interactions and scripting the conversation can be incredibly valuable. Use Kaizen to break this process down and, as a first step, complete a script for scheduling appointments. Create scripts for scheduling both routine appointments as well as emergency appointments. Assign the team member that is currently engaging patients to create these scripts and then review and modify them to create your message. All routine, recurring patient conversations should be scripted. At each staff meeting, review one or two scripts to keep them fresh and up-to-date.

Shape first impressions by critically looking at the appearance of your waiting room and furniture. Remember that the physical appearances of your team members and doctors will be used in assessing and creating a first impression. Practice brochures and other materials given to the patient, including health history and demographic forms, are also tangible evidence and help shape first impressions.

Manage Trust

Patients must trust your dental team because they have to purchase the service before they actually receive the service. A wax up of the final solution may help bridge the gap and increase trust levels. Smile design software may be used to facilitate the same net effect. Practice promotion videos, before and after pictures of patients actually treated, as well as testimonials also increase trust levels. Get to know what your patients want, what their dental goals are, who they are, and what makes them tick. These things all help build trust and show your patient you care about who he or she is as a person, not just a set of teeth. If you can discover three emotional wants or needs patients have and provide a connection by showing how a dental service will satisfy those wants and needs, your case acceptance rate will sky rocket.

Facilitate Quality Service

A quality appearance does not mean expensive or elegant, but rather clean and orderly with customer friendly appearances and systems. Small details that others overlook can promote a stronger message of caring and competence. This can be difficult. Spoken words are usually not enough to convey your message. A visual change is typically required as well.

Providing Sensory Stimulation

Architecture can be useful, but it is more important that your practice's ambiance, systems, and employee attitudes and appearance build on the message you desire to send. Practices need to control the sights, sounds, and smells in all areas of their practices including their waiting rooms, operatories, and bathrooms.

Socializing Employees

Your team members must be informed about your practice's marketing strategy and be able to help develop the look and feel of your practice. They must know, and preferably help create, the vision and mission statements of your practice and help modify these as time progresses.

Kaizen Action Plan/Check List

☐ Are you and your team sufficiently mindful that everything patients can sense is evidence about the service you provide? All the small things add up to the complete experience for your patients.

☐ Are you proactive in managing the tangible evidence?

☐ Does your practice manage the details well?

☐ Do you incorporate evidence management into your marketing plan?

☐ Do you use research to guide your management decisions?

☐ Do you spread ownership of evidence management throughout your practice?

☐ Does your team look for small changes to improve your evidence management throughout the organization in a consistent and ongoing manner?

☐ Is there any originality in what you do?

☐ Does your practice manage first impressions well?

☐ Do you invest in your employees' appearances?

☐ Do you manage evidence for your team members?

☐ Do tangibles in the work environment display concern or lack of concern for team members?

Branding Your Practice

A special form of tangible evidence for your practice is a branding tool. The essential purpose of branding is to distinguish your practice from another. Names, slogans, symbols, and uniforms help create a brand. The service you provide reinforces the intended brand image. However, please keep in mind that no matter how strong brands are, they cannot compensate for weak service.

Branding the Company

Branding can provide a marketing edge when patients perceive competitors to be similar. Branding is effective when a patient has little or no experience with the competing practices and responds to the strongest brand. Strong brands will help patients to visualize, understand, and believe in the service. Strong brands reassure patients.

The Name, The Core

The name of your practice must be distinctive and relevant and it must highlight the nature or benefit of your practice. It must be memorable and flexible. Brands are more than names --- They are the effective blending of all communication into a cohesive image. Graphic images can help. Slogans can also add power. Maximizing the effectiveness of the brand requires creativity to tell a meaningful story through a variety of elements and discipline to tell only one story.

Guidelines for Building a Strong Brand

There are three guidelines for building a strong brand: (1) research; (2) selecting the right medicine; and (3) internalizing the brand.

Start with Research

Begin the branding of your practice by asking small questions Kaizen style. What is the practice's current brand meaning to patients and team members? This is an important place to start. Next ask yourself how your practice's brand meaning compares to those of your key competitors. Geography is important in identifying your competitors. Also important is how well your company's name meets the test of a good name. What is important about your practice's service that could be conveyed by the brand? When branding your practice, you need to know your reason for existence. What is your niche? What is your "hedgehog concept?" Once you have identified your practice's meaning, it then needs to be conveyed in your brand.

Select the Right Medicine

Do not try to fix poor service with a strong brand. First fix the poor service through service error recovery as previously addressed and then develop a strong brand to help reinforce strong service.

Do not change a mediocre name when a strong brand exists already. Do not change a mediocre name even if it is somewhat flawed and sacrifice years of name recognition. Instead, build on what exists. Continuously improve your brand in small, consistent ways. This is much more effective than complacency followed by bursts of branding. Use the Kaizen way for small incremental branding efforts.

Internalize the Brand

Employees can be the most powerful medium for conveying the brand. They breathe life, vitality, and personality into the brand. Therefore, explain and sell the brand internally to your team members. Your team needs to understand and believe in the brand and then act it out.

Kaizen Action Plan/Check List

☐ Are you proactive in presenting a strong practice brand to your patients? Do you talk about branding at the management level? In staff meetings? In the operatories? Everywhere?

☐ How does your practice name rate in distinctiveness, relevance, memorability, and flexibility? Should it be changed/modified?

☐ Do you fully utilize branding elements other than the company name such as symbols, slogans, and perhaps audio?

☐ Is the presented brand cohesive? Is the brand both visual and verbal?

☐ Does your practice present your brand consistently across all media?

☐ Do you use all possible media to present your brand? Does your practice tap every opportunity to show and tell?

☐ Do you know what your brand means to your patients and staff and why?

☐ Does your practice internalize your brand?

Marketing to Current Patients

Your practice can increase its market share by:

1. Attracting more patients.
2. Doing more business with current patients.
3. Reducing patient attrition.

Direct marketing to existing patients takes care of two of the three listed above --- doing more business with your current patients and decreasing the chances of attrition of patients. Actions that the practice takes to nurture, build, and strengthen relationships with patients are crucial to marketing effectiveness and efficiency.

Creating Truer Patients

Relationship marketing will develop and retain patient relationships. Long term, or true, patients are the most profitable. They spend more money and stay with the practice the longest. They also spread favorable word-of-mouth information, which is a free form of advertising and lowers your practice's marketing cost.

Patients benefit as well from relationship marketing. Patients want the practice to contact them, rather than having to initiate contact. Therefore, call your patients for hygiene follow-ups and unfinished treatment. Know that patients want a partner, someone who cares for them, and someone who knows them. Call them like you would call a friend and ask them how you can assist them in achieving the dental care, condition, and confidence they would like to obtain.

Finances may be a significant barrier to your current patients. Consider establishing pre-payment plans. With these plans, patients set up automatic withdrawals from bank accounts or charges to credit cards by your practice. These funds are used to create a balance/credit on their account that can and will be used for dentistry in the future. Use Kaizen and have patients start by contributing small weekly or monthly amounts to their accounts. Then call your patients after six weeks and request their permission to increase the amount of their regular contribution. Repeat this call six-eight weeks later and everyone will be surprised how the account balance will increase. Unique companies like American HealthCare Lending™ (see Appendix B) can assist your patients with financing their procedures, thereby increasing case acceptance.

From People to Patients

Attracting new patients requires the slow, plodding work of building trust and relationships to move new patients to true patients of the practice who are above the line and ready to accept comprehensive dental care. Today's accounting does not fully reflect the true value of existing versus new patients.

Three Levels of Relationship Marketing

Level 1: Level 1 uses pricing to create incentive. Price incentives are easy for your competitors to imitate and therefore do not create a long term competitive advantage.

Level 2: Level 2 seeks to build social bonds on top of pricing bonds. This will not overcome significant pricing problems or service weakness, but it will encourage patients to remain in the absence of a strong reason to shift to a different practice.

Level 3: Level 3, relationship marketing, involves creating structural bonds that occur when the service provided is valuable and not easily available elsewhere. These services are often technology based and intended to help patients be more efficient and productive. The key is to provide value-added services that are difficult and expensive for patients to produce for themselves and hard to find elsewhere.

Trust

Trust is essential to building relationships and is built on fair play. Patients have needs that include realizing their objectives, being heard, receiving sensitive treatment when they are disclosing relevant information, and having promises kept. When you tell a patient that you are going to do something, do it. No matter how small the promise, it is vitally important that all promises are kept.

Making small promises and keeping them builds trust and can be part of an organized plan of building trust. After a comprehensive treatment planning session, the doctor can promise to call or have a staff member call that evening to answer any additional questions and help remove barriers facilitating patient care. This small promise and small action will bestow both small and big rewards for the doctor and team. When treating and dealing with patients, ask yourself not only which actions are legal and necessary, but also which are right. Without trust there is no comprehensive patient care.

One-on-One Marketing

Treat each patient as a market of one. Stay in touch and personalize the service for each patient. Access is fundamental to relationship building. Contact should be both practice and patient initiated, going both directions. Practice contact can assess patient perceptions of service, identify new desires or changes in desires, resell the benefits of services, and act as a vehicle to say thank you. Your practice needs to have organizational information and a means to efficiently tailor service to patients. The key to doing this efficiently is to institutionalize the process.

Consider assigning a team member to each patient as that patient's personal liaison. Give each patient their liaison's card as a personal contact in your practice. The personal liaison relationship should be reinforced with every patient visit, which will also allow for an orderly transition if a team member leaves your practice for any reason. If a team member does leave your practice, be sure to have a plan to transfer any patient calls for the departed team member to an experienced team member (rather than the new team member replacing the departed one).

Your practice's culture must not only make team members able to cater to your patients, but also desiring and willing to cater to their needs. This type of culture will be encouraged in your practice if you find ways to measure and reward success with catering to patients. Remember to keep the rewards small to preserve the satisfaction of a job well done.

Service Augmentation

Incorporate extras into the patient's experience. The trick is to identify extras that are valued by customers, not easily copied, and financially and operationally feasible. Service offerings that fit a practice's culture and foster social and structural bonding hold great potential.

Programs that entail improving patients' overall health and wellness are well received and valued highly by today's patient. A health and wellness program with smoking cessation and/or health and wellness products can be offered.

During a 30-minute after lunch appointment, create a system that shows your appreciation of your patients. For example, on the day of a significant treatment, a thank you card can be personalized and signed by the dentist and mailed 2-3 weeks after treatment. For cosmetic cases, before and after photos can be added. A reminder that you appreciate referrals is also a good idea.

Kaizen Action Plan/Check List

☐ Have you calculated the lifetime value of a patient and what effect patient defection has on your practice?

☐ Does your practice plan existing patient marketing, as well as new patient marketing?

☐ Does your practice stress value over price?

☐ Do you work hard to establish social bonds with your patients?

☐ Does your practice seek structural solutions to customer problems? Do you raise the cost to your existing patients of switching practices? Do you raise the benefits to potential patients of switching from your competitors?

☐ Do you prize fairness in your practice? When you make decisions, do you value fairness to the patient?

☐ Do you focus enough on competitive differentiation from other practices?

☐ Do you look for small ways to increase your connections to patients?

Marketing to Your Team

Effective patient marketing requires dental practices to have effective internal marketing that utilizes just as much imagination and vigor as patient marketing. Attracting, developing, motivating, and retaining qualified employees is paramount to practice success. Your ultimate goal should be to have team members who are willing and able to create true patients and raving fans. To do this, they must be raving fans as well.

Compete for Talent

One of the principle causes of poor service quality is hiring the wrong people to perform those services. Aim high and hire the right person and envision them performing the marketing tasks required. Develop ideal candidate profiles for each position. Involve your team members in the interviewing process and interview multiple times before filling a position. Look for a person that thrives on customer contact, as well as employees that can recruit other employees.

Offer a Vision

Attracting, developing, motivating, and retaining quality employees require a clear vision that is worth pursuing to them. You need to be passionate about your vision and convey that passion first to your team and then to your patients. Let your team members know how their work fits in the broader scheme of things. Your employees need to have a cause and feel needed in order to have passion for their work.

Your vision should be simple and communicated clearly at every opportunity by your practice's management. If management does not know the vision, who will? Take the time now to develop clear vision and mission statements. Keep them short and memorable so that you and your team can easily recall them at any time. Boil them down to essential elements that represent your practice and your culture. Avoid general statements such as: "We want to delivery high quality dentistry." This is not distinctive enough.

Consider holding a staff meeting to brainstorm key elements that define your organization. Then create possible statements from those key elements. Do not commit to a final statement until you have had a chance to reflect and rework the statement in private. Then re-present the mission and vision statements that you developed as a team. Revisit your statements yearly and modify them as necessary. Next, use your Kaizen skills to write down key action points that will take you closer to implementing your vision. Consistent small steps in the right direction will get you to the final destination in due time.

Prepare People to Perform

Give your employees both the skills necessary to perform ("the hows") and also give them "the whys." Knowledge and skill development is an ongoing process and not a sporadic event. When employees appear unmotivated, they likely lack confidence. Leadership positions should be filled with people who can teach others, be self-motivated, and enthusiastic.

Managers as Teachers: A New Mindset

Managers should also be teachers. A manager becomes a teacher when he or she moves from provider to patient orientation, from tolerance of the status quo to requiring higher standards, from director to empowerer, from employee as replaceable to employee as irreplaceable, from reactive to proactive, from tradition and safety to experimentation and risk, from front staff and back staff to team work across lines, and from cynicism to optimism. These are the makings of a manager who is also a teacher. Making these changes in your staff should, and can only, be done consistently in small increments. Creating new habits and paradigms is done by looking for and making small changes on a day-by-day and a week-by-week basis. This is the only way to create lasting and meaningful change that in the end is revolutionary.

Becoming a High Learning Practice

Commit to ongoing training and be guided by data. Discover weak areas and increase skills and knowledge in those areas. Use a mix of learning approaches with team members including audio, video, and role playing. Use role models and credible peers as examples. Institutionalize learning. Dedicate a portion of every staff meeting to learning. Take field trips to other offices and discuss the good and the bad features your staff observes at each office. Plan these field trips regularly, perhaps every 6-9 months. Evaluate and fine tune practice systems. Ask the team to list the changes that occurred after a specific training. Ask team members to take notes and come back from continuing educational courses and experiences with data and action points to implement in the practice. Learners that attend classes with the intent to later teach the information to others, learn the material better. Before the employee goes to a course, schedule the review and presentation about the course to occur shortly after he or she returns.

Stress Team Play

Service work is demanding, frequently frustrating, and sometimes demoralizing. It is common for service providers to become so stressed that they become less caring, less sensitive, and less eager to please. Team play is an anecdote for burnout. Use your next 30-minute time allotment to read the book *Fish! A Proven Way to Boost Morale and Improve Results* and learn about responsible play in the workplace and share the ideas with your team. Having a desire not to let the team down may be very motivating --- sometimes the most motivating factor for creating high and lasting performance.

Leverage the Freedom Factor

Humans are not meant to be robots and rule book management does not benefit the patient. Employees need some rules, but your practice should thin its rule book to bare essentials and build in values that guide decisions so few rules are needed. Along with this, empower employees and give them ownership of their success. Allow your team members to make decisions --- especially decisions that may be different from your decisions. Accept that there will be times when the wrong decision was made; however, the upside of engaged, empowered team members will far outweigh these moments. Be very careful when a bad decision is made and a correction must ensue. Use the moment as a teaching moment for the team and do not single out the team member who committed the infraction.

Empowerment

Employees may prefer to have everything spelled out in a comprehensive rule book, resisting a book with fewer rules. Managers may also resist having less control by allowing employees more freedom. Create a task force to go through the policy and procedures manual with the mandate to remove and modify rules that restrict service and employee freedom. Managers must be shown and re-shown the dangers of micromanagement and instead allow freedom and a widening of the solution boundaries for team members.

Measure and Reward

Internal marking efforts will be thwarted unless performance is measured and rewarded. Measuring systems must be direct and easy to implement and the rewards should be linked to the practice's vision and strategy. Make sure to distinguish between competence pay and performance pay. Keep rewards small in order to preserve the sense of accomplishment and the feeling of a job well done. Small rewards are much more effective in promoting continuous small changes throughout the practice. A large monetary reward implies a big idea with direct financial payback. Kaizen encourages small changes that may not immediately have a direct financial benefit, but in the end improve the practice and patient experience in great ways.

Charging a finance charge for overdue amounts is a small change that can have big results. The message that carrying a balance is not acceptable will change behaviors and decrease accounts receiveables.

Rewards

Use multiple rewards, including financial and nonfinancial recognition and career advancement. Remember the power of a pat on the back. Compete for the sustained commitment of employees. Stress the positive and reward achievements. Give everyone a chance. Reward teams and not just individuals. Five dollar gift certificates to local coffee or ice cream shops for creative small ideas will help accelerate the Kaizen process for change. Consider putting a one dollar bill down on the break room table at the morning huddle. Explain that this dollar will be rewarded to the person who comes up with the best example of a small process improvement for the day, or the best example of exceptional customer service for the day.

Know thy Patient

Ask team members about improvements, wants, desires, and needs of your team and patients. Create a periodic questionnaire for employees to give you this feedback. Summarize previous suggestions and actions taken from previous suggestions. Do not ask your employees for feedback unless you really want to hear their opinions and are willing to make changes. Otherwise you risk demoralizing your team and stifling creativity.

Kaizen Action Plan/Check List

☐ Do you compete as hard for employees and team members as you do for patients?

☐ Does your practice stand for something worthwhile?

☐ Do you prepare your people/team to perform with excellence?

☐ Do you stress team play? Do you allow your team to come through for your patients?

☐ Do you measure and reward what is important?

☐ Do you listen to your team? Do you first seek to understand?

☐ Do you connect with your team and with your patients consistently? As a matter of routine?

Retail Products

All practices should consider offering beneficial products to their patients in their offices. Offering products in dental, medical, chiropractic or surgical offices will become a standard in the future to provide additional benefits to their patients and to provide an additional source of income for the practice. By partnering with companies that offer unique products that are unavailable to people in standard retail fashion, practices can help patients to acquire products beneficial to them at the lowest possible prices. The key to make this successful is to offer products that add value to the patient's overall experience in your practice.

Choosing a Product

Deciding what product to offer is perhaps the key to making this successful within any practitioner's office. The product's brand must fit in nicely with the brand of the practice. If your practice has a high quality brand, then the products that you offer need to be of high quality as well. The products that you offer need to make sense and mesh well with the current environment or a future environment in a manner that will allow these products to have a natural place within your practice, practice culture, and systems. Without the natural ability to offer these products in day-to-day conversations in a routine fashion, the true power of offering products in your practice will be limited or lost.

Your team members, particularly the visionaries/practitioners/managers in your practice, need to be completely supportive of and passionate about the products you offer.

So, in summary, you need to pick a product that fits well with your practice brand, with your vision of your practice, and within your practice in a way that is easily discussed in your normal flow and day-to-day business either currently or in the future.

Network Marketing

Network marketing is using and selling products through word-of-mouth. Every doctor ideally wants to have happy patients that come to their office, have a fantastic experience, and go and tell all their family and friends about your practice resulting in their family and friends becoming patients of your practice. Network marketing uses the same concept to promote and sell products. Instead of spending money on television ads, radio ads, newsprint and magazine ads, network marketing companies invest the money they would spend on advertising on individuals that are promoting the company and introducing people to their products. The ideal practice in health care is based on word of mouth marketing, which is the exact same type of marketing as network marketing.

Often, practitioners are concerned that their patients will be turned off by the network marketing aspect of any particular company. This is a legitimate concern and should be addressed based on your patient population and based on how you offer the products to your patients. If your demographic patient population or geographical area is accepting of network marketing, particularly those in generations X and Y, this should be of little concern. With older patient population bases, offering the products without offering the network marketing component is a way to sidestep this potential barrier. What I mean by this is that you can offer the same products at either wholesale or retail prices and stay away from the network marketing or the business side of any particular product with patients that may resist the concept of network marketing.

Isagenix®

A good example of a company that has a series of products that can be offered within a dental or oral surgical practice is Isagenix®. Isagenix® is the perfect company for the vast majority of dental practices. This health and wellness company is dedicated to creating products of the utmost quality and transparency. I am currently implementing and using Isagenix® product sales in my practice, which consists of four doctors and three locations. I find this company's products fit in quite well with oral and maxillofacial surgical procedures and any other type of dental practice.

In our practice, we emphasize health and wellness and, through this emphasis, discuss the different avenues of product lines within the Isagenix® company. These products provide (1) exceptional value for our patients; (2) an internal bonus system for our staff members who choose to participate as Health and Wellness Coordinators; and (3) significant remuneration for the owners of our practice.

Benefits of Offering Isagenix® Products

There are many products available that can provide the following benefits to your patients:

1. Weight loss to help:
   - Improve obstructive sleep apnea.
   - Improve or eliminate type II diabetes.
   - Reduce or improve hypertension.

- Decrease the risk of heart attack and stroke.

2. Better nutrition and nutritional cleansing with products have helped people experience:
   - Increased energy.
   - Improved self-image and self confidence.
   - Increased athletic performance.

3. Meal Replacements:
   - Following extensive oral or surgical procedures, meal replacements allow for a liquid diet that is nutritional and nonchew.
   - Prior to extensive oral or surgical procedures, meal replacements provide proper nutrition, which improves healing and surgical results.
   - Convenient meal replacements with shakes or bars decrease the consumption of fast food, improving nutrition and saving money.

Offering these products can also provide the following benefits to your practice and your team:

1. The satisfaction of seeing improved health and wellness for your patients including

improved systemic and oral health in dental patients.

2. The satisfaction of providing comprehensive patient care.

3. A significant additional source of income for the practice.

4. A significant source of extra bonus money for the entire team.

5. High quality products improve the level of care for your patients and the brand of your practice.

6. As an optional benefit, you may choose to leverage the power of time in patients enthusiastic about the products you offer if they wish to pursue the business aspect of the product through network marketing.

Practitioners are often reluctant to offer products in their offices because of fear and anxiety and lack of previous experience. The fear and anxiety of offering products to patients in their office comes from the fear of rejection --- that patients will say "no." However, it is customary and typical to have patients say "no" to procedures that dentists may offer and dentists are used to accepting that. Having patients say "no" to products is also acceptable and should not be seen as a reason not to offer them. The office needs to see this as a sign that the full value of what they are offering is not being communicated well or that it's just not the right time.

Practitioners also avoid offering products that are sold through network marketing because of their lack of experience with network marketing and previous biases against it due to inaccurate information.

Your practice should consider offering products that are sold through network marketing.

Offering products in your office that are easily available through standard retail locations at competitive prices is quite difficult. This is where using network marketing companies really become beneficial for practitioners and patients.

Utilize Health and Wellness Coordinators

Health and Wellness Coordinators are staff members that are fully trained, or are in the process of being trained, about the products that you are selling within your office. They must be people who are passionate about the products, should be comfortable talking with patients and people, and be very customer service oriented. The benefits of being a Health and Wellness Coordinator are great and include not only financial rewards, but also the personal satisfaction of helping and assisting patients with beneficial products that will augment their treatment and/or care with your practice.

Implementing Retail Products in Your Practice

Before implementing any products into a practice, the major promoters in the practice, typically the doctors and/or office managers, need to overcome any potential negative attitudes and biases they may have toward network marketing. They must fully understand network marketing, notably that it is not a pyramid scheme. Most of us have had people in our lives compare network marketing to pyramid schemes and warn us to stay away from those schemes. Pyramid schemes are illegal and network marketing is not an illegal activity.

Pyramid schemes involve the transfer of money with no products exchanged or service rendered. Network marketing involves the sale and distribution of products and services in a completely legitimate and legal fashion and has been sometimes misunderstood and misrepresented as a pyramid scheme. Network marketing is a completely transparent activity to both the legal authorities and to the Internal Revenue Service. It is not illegal or immoral and should not be misconstrued in a negative fashion. Unfortunately, there are some network marketers that have promoted their products through pushy, intrusive, unprofessional ways, which has also served to give network marketing a bad reputation.

After overcoming personal biases and negative thoughts toward network marketers and their products, the next step is to find a product that fits well within your dental practice. This product has to represent your practice with the same kind of quality and character that is your practice's brand. It also needs to be something that the practice's owners and promoters of the products can be passionate about and have a strong belief in.

The next step is to personally experience the products you choose to create your own story. Creating your own story involves trying out the products, determining the results of those products, and examining how those products impacted your life and lifestyle.

Then you are ready to develop a plan of implementation for offering these products in your practice. This plan includes determining who these products would be best suited for and in what situations these products will be best used. In this way, you will identify your target audience for these products. In short, create a Kaizen style service blueprint mapping out implementation of product offerings.

After developing a plan of implementation, you will be ready to start training yourself and others on the best way to introduce these products to your target patients in a professional way that shows the benefits and added value of these products to your patients' overall experiences.

Training Yourself

Training yourself on how to offer the products you've chosen begins with your personal experience with the products. The network marketing company you choose will have training modules, which are usually internet based, to help you train yourself through a series of videos and information packages. If you are fortunate, you may also receive assistance from someone that has previous experience training his or her own office. This type of training can be very beneficial and can rapidly accelerate your success with this type of marketing. It can also create synergy between offices.

Training Your Team

You should first identify designated Health and Wellness Coordinators among your staff members. After you have trained yourself, you can begin training your team by starting with your Health and Wellness Coordinators. Your coordinators should learn the products and establish their own experiences with them.

It is best to ask your individual coordinators to purchase the products on their own in order to fully experience them without your influence. If employees use their own money to experience these products, the benefit is that this will greatly assist your practice in its ultimate implementation and acceptance of these products. When people acquire things and products at no cost to them, they are less committed to the full experience of the products and are less likely to develop their own story in a passionate way.

Scripting Your Sales

Any significant patient interaction in your practice should be scripted in detail and the employees that are involved in each interaction should be trained on the key elements of the scripts. Whenever introducing sales of your practice's product line, having specific scripts as to discussions about the products and how to relate the value of those products in the context of your practice is extremely important. Fortunately, companies like Isagenix® have amazing websites that are full of information and assistance.

(See www.bryanmclelland.isagenix.com for a fantastic example of a website that has fantastic training tools available for everyone.)

A key Kaizen action point here would be to create scripts for the five interactions in your office that are most likely to involve the product that you are introducing. For purposes of the following script examples, Isagenix® products will be used as the product examples.

Scenario One: A patient presents for a preoperative consultation involving an oral surgical/ dental procedure to be performed.

Dentist to Patient: During your oral surgical procedures, you will have a significant period of time where you will be on a soft, nonchew liquid diet. To assist you with this, we have some specific meal replacements and recommendations that include Isalean® shakes. We have partnered with this fantastic health and wellness company, and I have personally tried these products myself. These shakes/meal replacements are all liquid and will provide the necessary nutrients required during the healing process particularly with protein and other essential nutrients. A lot of research was done into different liquid meal replacements and products available and there is no other product available like this on the market. You can purchase the products through the internet, but because of our partnership with the company, you can get the lowest prices available through our practice saving 20-30%. If you would like any additional information or wish to order this, please let one of our Health and Wellness Coordinators know at your earliest convenience so that we can order these products and have them available on the day of your procedure.

Scenario Two: A patient completes a health history questionnaire and answers questions regarding whether he or she is on a diet or is interested in improving his or her health and wellness.

Dentist to Patient: Mr. Jones, what diet are you currently participating in? What has your success been with this diet? It is important to have adequate nutrition during the dieting process and this may or may not provide the adequate nutrition to be in the optimal health prior to your proposed procedures. Using the Isagenix® weight loss products for weight loss will ensure excellent nutrition and achieve very desirable results including not just the release of excess weight through a detoxifying process, but also a change in body dimensions and measurements. I personally experienced a 10-pound weight loss with their 9-day system/pack.

Scenario Three: A patient completes a health history questionnaire and answers questions regarding whether he or she is an athlete or interested in increasing his or her physical performance.

Dentist to Patient: Mr. Jones, I see that you have checked off that you are an athlete and interested in increasing your athletic performance. We have just introduced and partnered with a company, a whole nutritional and health and wellness product line, that has specific packs for athletes that can help increase their athletic performance. These products are for people looking for a competitive edge in their athletic endeavors through increased performance, as well as decreased recovery times after athletic exertions. If you are interested in additional information on these products and what we have available through our office, please inquire with one of our Health and Wellness Coordinators.

Scenario Four: After being introduced to the products, a patient has an objection or concern about the cost of the products.

Dentist to Patient: Mr. Jones, I understand exactly how you feel about the cost of these products. I also felt that when I was first introduced to these products, but what I found is that the cost of these products, at approximately $3-4 per meal, is far more economical than any fast food and most other meals that you would have during these times with nutrition that far exceeds those other options. I think many people find that their grocery bills are greatly reduced and that these products, when fully implemented, may actually save them money. Regardless of whether that is the case, the products are, at the least, very economical because meal replacement costs may decrease expenditures in your overall food bill.

Scenario Five: A patient wonders whether the products are good for diabetics, patients with hypertension, or patients with high cholesterol.

Dentist to Patient: Mr. Jones, the Isalean® shakes and Isagenix® bars are balanced in a 40-30-30 ratio with 40% of the calories coming from protein, 30% coming from carbohydrates, and 30% coming from healthy fats. This is what the American Diabetic Association recommends in well-balanced ADA approved diets. The complex nature of the carbohydrates and the high protein content of these meal replacements make control of glucose levels very predictable.

Author's Advice

I am very excited for anyone considering offering products in this fashion. This is likely to outstrip their current income through their normal practice given the power of time and numbers. Multiple offices working together can create synergy, taking the power of introducing products in this way and multiplying the effect exponentially. I would recommend contacting an office that is currently offering products from network marketing companies. I offer an invitation to you, the reader, to contact me at my e-mail address in the back of this book or my phone number to get additional inside information and training on how to implement products such as Isagenix® in your office at no cost.

Getting Started

Get started offering products in your practice by following these steps:

1. Isolate and identify a company that has products that you best envision fitting into your practice, visions, and branding.

2. Contact someone that currently uses the products you have identified in their office and has already developed systems and a model. This will allow you to leverage off their experience as well as to leverage off increased synergy with multiply linked practices and offices. I would like to extend the offer to anyone interested to contact me at my e-mail address or phone number for these purposes.

3. Implement the systems and educate your team as necessary to fully implement the product offerings in your office. Expect setbacks. Expect that small tweaks in your plan will need to occur over time. Have patience to allow the power of time to show

you the full benefits of implementing this type of model within your practice. With the diligence and skill that you have put into your training and practice, this will be a celebrated addition that will be quite beneficial to your patients, to your team, and to you.

Kaizen Action Plan/Check List

☐ Do you understand that there is no difference between network marketing and the desired way to market a successful practice through word of mouth?

☐ Evaluate your belief systems in the process of network marketing and embrace the system.

☐ Have you found a product and company that represent the quality and brand of your practice? Are you passionate about that company?

☐ Are you a product of the product? Consumable products and health and wellness products should be embraced and used by members in the practice.

☐ Are you partnered with an office that is experienced in offering these products to patients in a respectful and successful way?

☐ Have you created a blueprint for implementation of the product offering? Use your assigned time to do so.

☐ Use your resources upline and online to begin offering products to patients.

☐ Do you have scripts and changes in your health history form to help control and stimulate conversations?

☐ Do you understand the massive money making opportunity available that will likely outstrip your income as a healthcare provider due to leveraging the power of time and product/brand loyalty for both you and, just as importantly, for your team?

☐ Are you offering the products with the heart of service because you know the products can help your patients? Be sure your intentions and motivations are clear to you and appropriate.

☐ Set a goal of covering the cost of the product(s) you wish to consume monthly by generating cash offering products in your practice. Establish total monthly cash flow required to take some pressure off at home. $300? $500? $1,000? Celebrate when you hit these goals. Next determine the total monthly cash flow you require to live your dreams. $3,000? $5,000? $10,000? $25,000? Now determine how much per month you need to generate to feel like you are making progress toward the goal(s) you have set thus far. Write this number down. Allow five years to pass before you give up. Find your "why" and create the "how" to get to your "when" and achieve your dreams.

☐ Please feel free to email me at bryanmclelland@spokaneomfs.com if you would like specific information and coaching with Isagenix® and the systems my practice has put in place.

Conclusion

Making small changes on a consistent basis to move your practice and team forward is the most predictable and pleasant way to achieve success. Marketing a dental practice takes dedication, thought, and planning. The ideas in this book are tried and true and presented in a way that allows the culture of a practice to change and progress toward the final goal.

Kaizen is a practical philosophy that can be used to gradually implement changes in a practice. This method involves thinking small thoughts, asking small questions, taking small actions, solving small problems, bestowing small rewards, and identifying small moments.

You can use Kaizen to create a culture in your practice that will allow you to improve your team's service level, improve your practice's marketing, improve your practice's profitability, and increase both you and your team's enjoyment in practicing dentistry. Use the following Final Kaizen Action Plan/Checklist to ensure and realize that you have implemented all the evaluations and changes in your practice recommended in this book to achieve these goals.

This approach will decrease the stress associated with change by breaking it up into components so small that they seem easy and perhaps even trivial. Kaizen can help the leaders in your practice bypass the adrenaline-filled, fear producing path sometimes caused by innovative change by creating, fostering, and allowing gradual incremental change. These changes will lead to the practice of your dreams that will fulfill your desires and your team's desires and take your practice to the next level.

Enjoy the process and enjoy the journey.

Kaizen Action Plan/Check List

☐ Are you committed to providing service in your practice with 100% reliability?

☐ Is everyone on your team committed to providing service in your practice with 100% reliability?

☐ Have you created a blueprint designing your ideal practice?

☐ Have you established a brand for your practice?

☐ Have you established a regular biweekly or weekly staff meeting?

☐ Do you have the right people in the right positions on your team?

☐ Have you established a culture of teamwork in your practice?

☐ Have you evaluated all of the tangible aspects of your practice from a patient perspective?

☐ Do you have a system to capture patient complaints?

☐ Do you have a system to effectively resolve patient complaints?

☐ Have you begun selling retail products in your practice?

☐ Do you continuously monitor and evaluate all aspects of your practice to maintain a commitment to a high level of service?

Resources

Berry, Leonard and A. Parasuraman. (1991). *Marketing Services: Competing for Quality*. New York, NY: The Free Press.

Collins, Jim. (2010). *Good to Great: Why Some Companies Make the Leap...and Others Don't.* New York, NY: HarperBusiness.

Maurer, Robert. (2004). *One Small Step Can Change Your Life: The Kaizen Way.* New York, NY: Workman Publishing Company.

About the Author

Bryan W. McLelland, DDS, BSc is a practicing dentist and partner in Spokane Oral and Maxillofacial Surgery in Spokane, Washington. His practice services the Inland Northwest, including Eastern Washington and Northern Idaho, and offers comprehensive Oral and Maxillofacial Surgery procedures.

Dr. McLelland graduated from dental school at the University of Alberta in Edmonton in 1995, completed a one-year General Practice Residency at Denver General Hospital in Denver, Colorado from 1995-1996, and then received four years of specialized training in Oral and Maxillofacial Surgery at Cook County Hospital in Chicago, Illinois.

He is a member of the following professional associations: American Dental Association; American Association of Oral and Maxillofacial Surgeons; American Society of Dental Anesthesiology; The International Association of Oral and Maxillofacial Surgeons; The American Academy of Osseointegration; Western Society of Oral and Maxillofacial Surgeons; The Spokane District Dental Society, American College of Oral and

Maxillofacial Surgeons, and Spokane Chamber of Commerce.

Dr. McLelland's practice is dedicated to providing exceptional customer service with an unparalleled level of empathy and care. He is committed to assisting dentists across the country in gaining a competitive edge in their local markets through improved marketing practices and service levels; thereby increasing their profitability and enjoyment in practicing dentistry.

Dr. McLelland is also available for speaking engagements on the topics of marketing dental practices, dental implants, and oral and maxillofacial surgical procedures.

In addition to practicing dentistry, Dr. McLelland has partnered with Isagenix®, a health and wellness company, to provide his patients and staff improved health and financial benefits.

If you would like to consult with Dr. McLelland about improving your practice and its marketing, or about offering retail products such as Isagenix® in your practice, he is available at bryanmclelland@spokaneomfs.com.

Spokane Oral and Maxillofacial Surgery

Spokane Oral & Maxillofacial Surgery provides oral surgery and facial cosmetic surgery services in two offices in Spokane, Washington and one in Post Falls, Idaho. Oral surgery procedures offered include dental implants, wisdom teeth, tooth extraction, repair of facial injuries, jaw surgery, and biopsies.

Oral and Maxillofacial Surgery requires 4-6 additional years of hospital based surgical and anesthesia training. As Oral and Maxillofacial Surgeons, **Dr. Paxton, Dr. Lang, and Dr. McLelland** manage a wide variety of problems relating to the mouth, teeth and facial Regions. They practice a full scope of Oral and Maxillofacial Surgery with expertise ranging from Cleft Lip and Palate Surgery Cosmetic Facial Surgery to Corrective Jaw Surgery and Wisdom Tooth Removal. All doctors can also diagnose and treat patients with chronic Facial Pain, Facial Injuries and TMJ disorders, and perform a full range of Dental Implant procedures.

Spokane Oral & Maxillofacial Surgery offers the only dual accredited Ambulatory Surgical Center (ASC) for Oral & Maxillofacial Surgery in the Inland Northwest. SOMFS is accredited by the Accreditation Association for Ambulatory Health Care (AAAHC) and the Joint Commission for Accreditation of Healthcare Organizations.

Contact Information:

800.221.7106
509.926.7106
www.spokaneomfs.com

Isagenix® is a health and wellness company dedicated to restoring and revitalizing the body's systems to promote good health. Its cutting-edge products include essential nutritional supplements, dietary health, and skincare products and are made of only high-quality, natural ingredients. Its research and development team ensures that ingredients are safe, pure, and potent.

If you are interested in improving your health, increasing your energy levels, improving your athletic performance, and/or losing weight, Isagenix® can help!

Isagenix® is also dedicated to improving the lives of its associates through financial freedom with its management and compensation systems.

For more information about this amazing company and the opportunities it offers, see www.bryanmclelland.isagenix.com or contact Dr. Bryan McLelland at: bryanmclelland@spokaneomfs.com.

Isagenix® Customers

Ken Simpson (Before)   Ken Simpson (After)

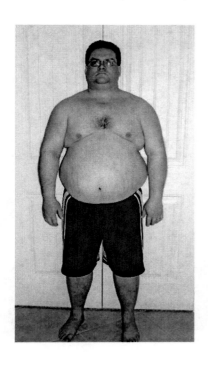 

Joni Brewer (Before)   Joni Brewer (After)

Isagenix® Products

INDEPENDENT ASSOCIATE

Nutritional Cleansing

Be clean, lean and energized with Nutritional Cleansing!

Many people have been amazed by their results from Nutritional Cleansing, experiencing:
- Greater vitality
- Improved focus
- Better physical fitness
- The ability to maintain healthy weight

Greater energy and a healthy weight is within reach—go for it today by visiting www.bryanmclelland.isagenix.com or contact Dr. Bryan McLelland at: bryanmclelland@spokaneomfs.com!

These statements have not been evaluated by the FDA. These products are not intended to diagnose, treat, cure or prevent any disease.

Ionix® Supreme

Instantly improve performance and ease stress with nutrients

Ionix® Supreme, the premium formula from Isagenix®, is created with high-quality nutrients to help your body:
- Better cope with the effects of stress
- Improve physical and mental performance
- Support immune health

Adaptogens, antioxidants and whole food concentrates are blended in Ionix® Supreme to help you make a huge leap forward in health and fitness.

Experience it for yourself by visiting
www.bryanmclelland.isagenix.com
or contact Dr. Bryan McLelland at:
bryanmclelland@spokaneomfs.com **today!**

These statements have not been evaluated by the FDA. These products are not intended to diagnose, treat, cure or prevent any disease.

For Our Children's Health

Isagenix® has taken the lead in providing unparalleled nutritional products for children to help them obtain optimal wellness.

Find out more by visiting
www.bryanmclelland.isagenix.com
or contact Dr. Bryan McLelland at:
bryanmclelland@spokaneomfs.com **today!**

These statements have not been evaluated by the FDA. These products are not intended to diagnose, treat, cure or prevent any disease.

124

GETAWILLNOW.COM

GETAWILLNOW.COM is a website designed to allow healthcare professionals and other individuals to create a valid Last Will and Testament in an expeditious, user-friendly, and inexpensive way. This website is for you if you have a net worth of less than $2 million and need a basic will that:

- Names an executor for your estate.
- Leaves your property to your designated beneficiaries.
- Names a guardian for your children.
- Names someone to manage your finances and property for your underage children.

GETAWILLNOW.COM also allows healthcare professionals to specify the orderly transition of a practice, but is subordinate to the practice operational agreements that may already be in place.

The difference between GETAWILLNOW.COM and other sites that offer the same service is that your legal will is stored online in our E-Vault. You have the ability to access and modify the contents of your will at any time, day or night, so that your will can always be kept up-to-date!

Additionally, GETAWILLNOW.COM donates ten percent (10%) of all proceeds to charity. Helping yourself now helps others.

Protect your family and your loved ones. Please go to www.getawillnow.com and create your last will and testament now!

Appendix A

NuCalm™

236B Junction Hwy
Kerrville, TX 78028
Phone: 877.668.2256
www.nucalm.com

Overview*

NuCalm™ is a revolutionary technology proven to naturally relax the body within minutes without drugs. This new technology improves the dental experience for clinicians, dental teams, and patients by providing a fully relaxed and comfortable dental experience for every patient. It is safe, predictable, reliable, easy to use, and patients will not experience any side effects or required recuperation time.

Developed by a pioneering neuroscientist in Kerrville, Texas, NuCalm™ was launched into the dental industry after eight years of research and scientific discovery, product development, and clinical validation. To date, over 32,400 dental patients across the U.S. have experienced a relaxing dental appointment with NuCalm.

NuCalm™ is sophisticated neuropsychobiology and neurobioinformatics applied in a simple clinical solution that naturally brings the brain wave function to the first stage of sleep. A person in the first stage of sleep is physically unable to have an anxious response and exhibits deep breathing, relaxed facial muscles, relaxed body posture, and dulled resistance mechanisms – reduced salivary flow, reduced tongue movement, and reduced gag reflexes.

NuCalm™ transforms every patient into the ideal patient - fully relaxed and fully cooperative during the procedure. With NuCalm™, clinicians can focus exclusively on dentistry.

Patient Anxiety

Anxiety is caused by a biological response to the stimulus of a threat, real or perceived. When a person is faced with a threat, the amygdala prepares the body by contacting an array of brain regions to activate the fight-or-flight system. The fight-or-flight response uses the sympathetic nervous system and the adrenal-cortical system to alert the body to speed up, tense up, become hypervigilant, and take action. The sympathetic nervous system triggers the release of epineph-rine (adrenaline) and norepinephrine (noradrenaline) from the adrenal medulla into the bloodstream. These hormones increase heart rate and blood pressure. In parallel, the hypo-thalamus releases corticotropin-releasing factor (CRF) into the pituitary gland, which triggers the release of the adrenocorticotropic hormone (ACTH). ACTH travels through the blood stream to the adrenal cortex where it initiates the release of numerous hormones that prepare the body to respond to a threat.

The physiology of anxiety is characterized by cognitive, somatic, emotional, and behavioral components. These components combine to cre-ate feelings of fear, apprehension, and/or worry. Anxiety is often accompanied by physical sensa-tions such as heart palpitations, nausea, chest pain, shortness of breath, stomach ache, cold and clammy feeling extremities, irritability, muscle tension, or headache.

Impact of Anxiety in America

Anxiety is as common an emotion as fear, anger, sadness, and happiness, and it has an important function in relation to human survival. However, anxiety can become maladaptive resulting in neurosis or phobias. Generalized Anxiety Disor-der (GAD) is the most common diagnosed mental illness in the U.S., affecting over 40 million adults and costing over $42 Billion in annual healthcare expenditures. According to the Anxiety Disorders Association of America (ADAA), $22.84 Billion of the annual costs are associated with the repeated use of healthcare services; people with anxiety disorders seek relief for symptoms that mimic physical illnesses.

A specific phobia is an intense, irrational fear of something that poses little or no actual danger. The DSM-IV describes dental phobia as a "marked and persistent fear that is excessive or unreasonable." While Humans are anthropologically conditioned to protect their mouth as a means to survival and anxious dental patients are physically programmed to challenge the procedure as an act of survival. Adults with phobias realize these fears are irrational, they often find that facing, or even thinking about facing, the feared situation brings on a panic attack or severe anxiety.

Anxiety acutely affects most Americans when they have medical procedures ranging from dentistry to dialysis to chemotherapy. An anxious body is more resistant to treatment and can compromise the effectiveness of the treatment. An anxious mind, in many cases, may avoid seeking treatment thus compromising good health and quality of life. With NuCalm™, people can now get the healthcare they need without the anxiety commonly associated with medical treatment.

Impact of Anxiety in the Dental Market

NuCalm™ is a clinical solution with broad applications addressing the human condition of anxiety and stress through the natural communication pathways of the midbrain. We launched NuCalm™ into the U.S. dental industry first due to latent demand...most people don't want to be in a dental chair. In fact, 82% of adults report some level of anxiety about dentistry and approximately 60M Americans avoid the dentist entirely. There is extensive research regarding the oral systemic health link and the negative impact neglecting oral health can have on a human being. Anxiety is a profound problem that negatively impacts dental patient experiences.

Dental patient anxiety is caused by several subjective stimuli including fear of pain, fear of needle injections, fear that the injection/anesthesia won't work, fear of anesthetic side effects, sense of helplessness, and fear of embarrassment/shame in the cases of neglected oral healthcare. Anxiety is not a positive experience for patients or dentists and this unmet need continues to demand a solution.

The Impact of Dental Anxiety on the Clinician

As one clinician points out, "It's a battle. When I'm working on anxious patients, I'm always on defense. I never get to play offense, and do my best clinical work." The bottom line is, the patient is not in control. Their body is consumed by their fight-or-flight response and they are simply trying to protect themselves. Clinicians must be able to manage their patient's behaviors and at the same time provide a high level of clinical care. This is a significant challenge if the patient cannot fully cooperate.

Neutralizing Anxious Patients with Sedation Techniques

Sedation techniques have become the most effective way to manage anxious patients. These include:
- Oral sedation (benzodiazepines)
- Intravenous (IV) sedation - typically using a combination of different drug classes
- Inhalation sedation (nitrous oxide)
- Oral Sedation

Benzodiazepines

Benzodiazepines provide powerful relief from the symptoms of anxiety by slowing down the central nervous system. Benzodiazepines act mainly through the GABA-A receptor subtype by potentiating GABA transmission. GABA (Gamma Aminobutyric Acid) is a ubiquitous neurotransmitter, involved in the majority of inhibitory synapses in the brain. Thus, GABA suppresses neural firing, inhibiting or regulating other neurotransmitters including serotonin, norepinephrine, and dopamine. It accomplishes this by decreasing their turnover in limbic areas - amygdala, locus ceruleus, and raphe nuclei.

The use of benzodiazepines to sedate anxious dental patients is a popular form of treatment. Benzodiazepines help anxious patients relax throughout the procedure but they force clinicians and their teams to act as part-time anesthesiologists. According to ADA guidelines, because sedation is a continuum, it is not always possible to predict how an individual patient will respond. Hence, practitioners intending to produce a given level of sedation should be able to diagnose and manage the physiologic consequences (potential rescue) for patients whose level of sedation becomes deeper than intended. For all levels of sedation, the practitioner must have the training, skills, drugs, and equipment to identify and manage such an occurrence until either assistance arrives (emergency medical service) or the patient returns to the intended level of sedation without airway or cardiovascular complications. The use of benzodiazepines can compromise the patient experiences and adds a level of complexity and risk for clinicians.

IV Sedation

IV sedation refers to anti-anxiety medication delivered intravenously. This form of sedation requires special training or an anesthesiologist present. The medications used for IV sedation are typically benzodiazepines, but can vary widely depending on patient needs. The doctor adjusts the dose until the patient is nearly unconscious - patients should be able to respond to commands to open mouth, turn head, swallow, etc. Depending on the medication used, IV sedation often results in a powerful amnestic experience.

Inhalation Sedation (Nitrous Oxide)

Nitrous oxide (N2O) is commonly used by clinicians to help sedate anxious and fearful patients. N2O is a weak anesthetic agent when used alone. It is often used in combination with local anesthesia as well as other sedative, hypnotic agents.

Common complaints by clinicians regarding nitrous oxide include the investment costs, time required at the end of the procedure to oxygenate patients, inconvenience of the mask in the way of clinician's hands, and inconsistent patient experiences. Nitrous oxide costs valuable chair time waiting for the patient to equilibrate their oxygen levels after the procedure and usually requires additional staff for the recovery period.

Impact of Using Sedation Techniques

Sedation techniques do provide a level of care that helps allay patient anxiety during a procedure. The challenge with using these techniques is the complexity, unpredictability, risk, and cost associated with these forms of patient care.

The Natural Solution: NuCalm™

NuCalm™ is a patent-pending, proprietary technology proven to relax the body within minutes by bringing alert beta brain wave function down to the alpha range (first stage of sleep characterized by brain wave frequencies between 8Hz-12Hz per second).

NuCalm™ leverages the synergistic benefits of four sensory applications: proprietary chewable tablets (natural anxiolytic neurotransmitters), CES (Cranial Electrotherapy Stimulation) to catalyze the effectiveness of the NuCalm™ neurotransmitters, neuroacoustic binaural beat software, and black-out glasses. NuCalm™ is unique because it creates deep relaxation without using narcotics or controlled substances, causes no side effects, and requires no recuperative time or supervision.

Before NuCalm™, patients had two ways to cope with the anxiety induced by a healthcare procedure: chemical sedation or avoid the treatment. With NuCalm™ clinicians can create a relaxed experience without the risks associated with conventional sedation techniques.

NuCalm™ organically entrains brain waves to a frequency that creates relaxation and calm. Beta brain waves (13 Hz-30 Hz) are associated with day-to-day wakefulness – mental activity consisting of cognitive, sensory and motor activities. High beta brain waves (23 Hz-40 Hz) are associated with fear and anxiety. NuCalm™ brings the patient's brain waves from beta or high beta to the alpha range (8 Hz-12 Hz). Alpha brain waves are associated with relaxation, meditation, and idleness. A patient with brain waves in the alpha range is physically unable to be anxious. NuCalm™ naturally entrains the brain to the alpha range, creating cellular homeostasis, neuromuscular release, and relaxation. Patients leave dental appointments feeling relaxed and rejuvenated.

The neurophysiologic manifestations of NuCalm™ include the following:
- Rapid induction of parasympathetic hypnogogic dissociative state
- Sustained, steady parasympathetic dominance throughout the procedure

- Rapid return to a functional state (motor skills, attention, and full cognition) with no lingering negative post-sedative effects

The NuCalm™ system includes four main components:
- Proprietary chewable tablets containing neurotransmitters that interfere with the fight-or-flight anxious response
- Cranial Electrotherapy Stimulation (CES) device
- Proprietary neuroacoustic software
- Black-out glasses
- Chewable Tablets

The NuCalm™ proprietary orthomolecular formula has been developed and engineered over several years to maximize the body's natural relaxation response with NuCalm™. The proprietary formula is only available in the NuCalm™ system and includes structured nutrient-sourced building blocks that rapidly enter the brain and convert to powerful messengers that suppress anxiety and create relaxation. The NuCalm™ chewable tablets work on the GABAergic system to counteract adrenaline and begin the relaxation response.

The primary ingredients include:
- Gamma-Aminobutyric Acid (GABA) – an inhibitory neurotransmitter that promotes a state of deep relaxation and calm
- L-Theanine – a free (non-protein) amino acid found almost exclusively in tea plants (Camellia sinensis). L-Theanine supports the formation of GABA.

GABA

GABA is a major inhibitory neurotransmitter that reduces the excitability of neurons. Over-stimulated or over-active neurons may lead to feelings of restlessness, irritability, and sleeplessness. GABA inhibits nerve cells from over-firing to promote feelings of calmness and stability.
CES studies show reduced rigidity in the central nervous system stimulation process and enhanced activity of the alpha-rhythm generating systems.

GABA is naturally produced from the amino acid glutamine and the sugar glucose. It is concentrated in the hypothalamus area of the brain and is known to play a role in healthy pituitary function, which helps maintain hormone synthesis, proper sleep cycles, and body temperature.

GABA is one of the only amino acids that can pass through the blood-brain barrier when administered orally. The GABA A and GABA B receptor sites are located in the same area as the brain receptor sites for benzodiazepines, barbiturates, and alcohol.

L-Theanine

L-Theanine is an amino acid that has been shown to induce a general calming effect. The natural effects of L-Theanine include:

- Stimulating the production of alpha brain waves
- Protecting and restoring the brain
- Inducing deep states of relaxation
- Up-regulating GABA – increasing its clinical efficacy and relaxation effect

Studies show that L-Theanine plays a role in inducing the same calm and feeling of well-being as meditation, massage, or aromatherapy.

Cranial Electrotherapy Stimulation (CES)

The Cranial Electrotherapy Stimulation (CES) device produces low amounts of electrical current (close to the cell's own electrical values – microcurrent is less than 1/1,000 of an Amp). This easy-to-use device has been cleared by the FDA for the treatment of anxiety, depression, and insomnia. Research over the past 50 years indicates an increase in metabolism of neurotransmitters as evidenced by an increase in the metabolites of the neurochemicals. Other research points to a normalization and balance of the brain's neurochemistry by reestablishing optimal neurotransmitter levels. Low-level electrical current interacts with cell membranes in a manner that produces modifications in information transduction associated with classical second messenger pathways. Electrical engineering studies found that a small fraction of CES current actually reaches the thalamic area of the brain facilitating the release of neurotransmitters.

Combining CES with precursor neurotransmitters causes a profound state of relaxation and anxiolysis. QEEG and EEG's indicate a brain wave shift occurring whereby the patient's brain activity slows down – from beta brain waves of high alertness to alpha brain waves that are present during a relaxed, pre-sleep state.

Neuroacoustic Software

The proprietary neuroacoustic software provided in the NuCalm system uses binaural beats and Frequency-Following-Response (FFR) that initiate a change in brain waves. According to extensive research, a scientifically validated neurophysiologic response is initiated when an auditory pacing signal is presented to the brain. We have developed significant advances in the design of binaural and monaural beat sound acoustics, which are overlaid with classical music and administered to the patient using an MP3 player and noise-dampening headphones.

The neuroacoustic brain entrainment software paces the patient's brain waves from the high beta brain wave frequencies associated with anxiety (23 Hz-40 Hz) to brain wave frequency patterns of alpha (primarily 8 Hz-12 Hz). These alpha brain waves are associated with deep relaxation and calmness.

Binaural beats are auditory brainstem responses, which originate in the superior olivary nucleus of each hemisphere. They result from the interaction of two different auditory impulses, originating in opposite ears, registering below 1,000 Hz and which differ in frequency between one and 30 Hz (Oster, 1973). For example, if a pure tone of 500 Hz is presented to the right ear and a pure tone of 510 Hz is presented simultaneously to the left ear, an amplitude modulated standing wave of 10 Hz, the difference between the two tones, is experienced as the two wave forms mesh in and out of phase within the superior olivary nuclei. This binaural beat is undetected by the ears (the human range of hearing is from 20-20,000 Hz). It is perceived as an auditory beat, and theoretically can be used to entrain specific neural rhythms through the frequency following response, thus modulating the brain wave frequency in the case of NuCalm™ to 8 Hz and 12 Hz.

Black-Out Glasses

The black-out glasses used in the NuCalm™ system block light from the optic nerve resulting in an immediate increase (up to 30%) in alpha waves in the occipital cortex of the brain. This helps maintain deep relaxation.

The NuCalm™ system combines several scientific and technological advancements that have been used to treat anxiety as standalone solutions. The clinical procedure takes approximately 3 minutes for patient setup and approximately 3-5 additional minutes before the patient experiences deep relaxation.

The patient experiences NuCalm™ for the duration of the dental procedure as the neuroacoustic software paces the patient's brain waves between 8 Hz and 12 Hz. Once the dental procedure is completed, the NuCalm™ components are removed and the patient will experience a relaxed, refreshed feeling with no side effects and no recuperative time needed.

To date, NuCalm™ has been used on over 32,400 dental patients across the United States without a single reported adverse experience.

To facilitate easy implementation, clinical proto-
cols have been developed, refined, and
documented into "best practices" training tools
for dentists and their teams. NuCalm™ can alle-
viate negative patient experiences that are caused
by fear and anxiety and can change the perceptions Americans have about going to the dentist.
Imagine the impact NuCalm™ can have on the
dental industry and the overall oral health of the
American population if dentists can provide relaxing and rejuvenating dental experiences.

NuCalm Effect

NuCalm™ profoundly affects the patient's well-
being. Their body will feel relaxed, their mind
will be at ease, and they will go about their day
feeling refreshed and rejuvenated. NuCalm™
mimics the natural communication pathways the
body uses to prepare for sleep. By providing a
"power nap" that is equivalent to nearly five
hours of restful sleep, NuCalm™ creates a neuro-
logical "reboot." NuCalm™ specifically addresses
the physiology of the midbrain stress and anxiety
response. A healthy body and brain requires balance between the sympathetic nervous system
and parasympathetic nervous system. Many people suffer the consequences of sympathetic
nervous system dominance – which results in
stress related illnesses and emotional fatigue.
NuCalm™ creates parasympathetic nervous sys-

tem dominance required to achieve deep relaxation of the brain and body.

NuCalm™ naturally interferes with the adrenaline/cortisol response associated with the midbrain activities of the fight-or-flight system. During the NuCalm™ experience oxygenated red blood cells pump through the entire body, removing lactic acid and creating cellular rejuvenation.

After a NuCalm™ experience people can expect the following:

- Their body will feel relaxed – their stress and muscle tension will be gone as the oxygenated red blood cells flush out the lactic acid in areas of physical tension. Their joints will feel loose and fluid, similar to how people feel after a deep tissue massage, minus the bruising.
- Their mind will feel at ease, as if they have no worries for a couple of hours. Often in times of stress, people say, "just sleep on it and you will feel better in the morning." With NuCalm™, the person has essentially "slept on it." This occurs as a direct result of halting the midbrain stress response while pumping oxygenated red blood cells through the pre-frontal cortex, hippocampus, and frontal cortex. The frontal cortex of the brain is where cognition exists – people's thoughts, ability to reason, and

144

processing of information. This is the same state physiologically, emotionally, and mentally, where people who meditate, practice mindfulness, or practice expert level yoga achieve. This is the healthy balance between mind and body.

- They will experience greater mental acuity and clarity of thought for several hours. The oxygenated red blood cell flow through the frontal cortex results in greater communication pathways. They will feel more creative and able to reason with enhanced clarity.
- They will sleep better after experiencing NuCalm™. They will feel more rested and sleepy around their usual bedtime and will experience deeper sleep for 1 to 2 nights. The GABAergic system is responsible for relaxing people and preparing them for sleep at night. NuCalm™ primes the GABAergic system resulting in healthy, all-natural sleep.

NuCalm™ Benefits

- Causes effective, safe anxiolysis where a relaxed state is induced and maintained for an entire procedure
- Minimizes risk to patient and clinician during a procedure – patient's motor responses are significantly reduced

- Promotes efficiencies for clinician because patients are relaxed and still (no startle responses and sudden patient movements; reduced salivary flow and gag reflexes)
- Is less intrusive than sedation techniques – does not chemically compromise the central nervous system or cognitively impair the patient's mind
- Patient's body is more receptive to treatment (natural resistance mechanisms are dulled)
- Patients can come and go on their own (there are no side effects, no recovery time or supervision needed, and no cognitive impairments)
- Patient's post-treatment experience is a feeling of rejuvenation and relief (NuCalm™ helps the brain achieve cellular homeostasis which provides a neuromuscular release of any bodily tension and a sense of balance through the increased flow of oxygenated red blood cells)
- Increased positive patient experiences – eventually will recondition patients to associate healthcare treatment with relaxation and rejuvenation

NuCalm™ Impact

- Increased patient referrals –increased positive patient experiences will motivate your patients to spread the word about your exceptional service

- Higher percentage of case acceptance; less patient fear and less anxiety = less barriers to "yes" for treatment and at-home oral health compliance; patients will schedule additional appointments and keep them
- Activate patients that have neglected their oral healthcare due to fear/anxiety (~60 Million Americans)
- Dentistry without compromise – increased procedural efficiencies by working on quiet, still patients
- Better schedule management – using Nu-Calm™ on every patient will free time in your schedule and help you respond to emergency cases
- Less stress – anxious patients create stressful work environments; when patients are relaxed, clinicians and team members are relaxed
- Less risk – the dental team does not need to act as part-time anesthesiologists, monitoring their patient's vital signs

Blueprint/Assistants Guide to Administering NuCalm™

1. Administer Chewable Tablets
   a. Step 1 Bottle: Have patient chew 1 tablet and keep in mouth for 1 minute before swallowing.
   b. Step 2 Bottle: Have patient chew 2 tablets and keep in mouth for 1 minute before swallowing.

2. Administer NeuroPax Device
   a. Attach lead wires to provided adhesive patches.
   b. Apply patches to the soft spot behind the ears just below the mastoid bone.
   c. Turn on NeuroPax device and keep at low intensity.
   d. Press the black "Timer" button 2 times until the green light above the "Continuous" is lit.
   e. Slowly increases intensity until the patient feels any sensation (scratchy, pulsing) and then decrease until the patient is comfortable.
   f. Place the NeuroPax device in provided pouch and hang on back or side of chair.

3.   Administer MP3 Player and Head-phones
     a. Turn on headphones (green light appears) and turn up volume to maximum level.
     b. Attach headphones to the MP3 player.
     c. Turn on the MP3 player and begin music at the beginning of track 1.
     d. Adjust volume to patient's comfort level. Note that the music should be loud and the patient should NOT be able to hear soft voice commands.
     e. Place MP3 player in the provided pouch with the NeuroPax device.

4.   Administer Light-Blocking Glasses
     a. Patient can choose between "blackout" glasses or sunglasses, depending on their comfort level.

5.   Removing NuCalm™ Components
     a. Ask patient to remove light-blocking glasses.
     b. Ask patient to remove headphones.
     c. Turn off headphones and MP3 player.
     d. Turn off NeuroPax device and remove patches from behind the patient's ears.

Patient's Commonly Asked Questions About NuCalm™

What is NuCalm™?

NuCalm™ is a safe, proven system that quickly and effectively relaxes you without using narcotics or controlled substances.

How does NuCalm™ work?

NuCalm™ has 4 components administered in approximately 3 minutes at the beginning of your appointment. First, you will be given chewable tablets to relax you by counteracting adrenaline. Second, you will receive micro current stimulation to open up communication pathways and receptors for relaxation. Next, you will get NeuroAcoustic software layered with soothing music and used with noise-dampening headphones. Last, you will wear black-out glasses to negate visual stimuli and help maintain relaxation.

Are the tablets and micro current stimulation safe?

The tablets are all natural concentrated from high protein foods such as turkey, mozzarella cheese and green tea. We have more information on exactly what is in the chewable tablets if you would like to see that.

The Cranial Electrotherapy Stimulation (CES) device has been cleared by the FDA for treatment of anxiety, depression and insomnia. The CES device produces low amounts of electrical current (close to the cell's own electrical values—micro current is less than 1,000,000th of an Amp).

Do I have to do them all together?
In order to get the full benefits of Nu-Calm™, it is recommended that all steps are followed.

What are the benefits of NuCalm™?
- Causes effective, safe anxiolysis where a relaxed state is induced and maintained for the patient's appointment
- Patient's body is more receptive to treatment (natural resistance mechanisms are dulled)
- Reduces patient's motor response—minimizing risk to patient and clinician during a procedure
- Patient is relaxed yet conscious and can respond to voice commands during a procedure
- Patients can come and go on their own (there are no side effects, no recovery time or supervision needed, and no impairments)

Brain Nutrients: Ingredients in Chewable Tablets

The NuCalm™ brain nutrients, a proprietary orthomolecular formula, are specifically designed to maximize the reduction in anxiety in the brain and central nervous system. The formula includes:

- Gamma-Aminobutyric Acid (GABA) – an inhibitory neurotransmitter that promotes a state of deep relaxation and calm
- L-Theanine – a free (non-protein) amino acid found almost exclusively in tea plants (Camellia sinensis). L-Theanine supports the formation of GABA.

GABA

GABA is a major inhibitory neurotransmitter that reduces the excitability of neurons. Over-stimulated or over-active neurons may lead to feelings of restlessness, irritability, and sleeplessness.

GABA is naturally produced from the amino acid glutamine and the sugar glucose. It is concentrated in the hypothalamus area of the brain and is known to play a role in healthy pituitary function, which helps maintain hormone synthesis, proper sleep cycles, and body temperature.

GABA is the only amino acid that can pass through the blood-brain barrier when administered orally. The GABA receptor site is located in the same area as the brain receptor sites for Benzodiazepines, barbiturates, and alcohol.

L-Theanine

L-Theanine is an amino acid that has been shown to induce a general calming effect. The natural effects of L-Theanine include:
- Stimulating the production of alpha brain waves
- Protecting and restoring the brain
- Inducing deep states of relaxation
- Up regulating GABA—increasing its clinical efficacy and relaxation effect

Studies show that L-Theanine plays a role in inducing the same calm and feeling of well-being as mediation, massage, or aromatherapy.

When and How NuCalm™ will be Administered at SOMFS

NuCalm™ can be offered to the patient who is anxious or nervous about their procedure because they can't or don't want to use general anesthesia. There are going to be some instances where the doctor will not advise NuCalm™ depending on the extent of the procedure.

When discussing the option of NuCalm™ with the patient and they should happen to have any questions, please refer to "Patient's Commonly Asked Questions About NuCalm™" document. There is also documentation on what exactly is in the chewable tablets that will be administered.

If the patient is still very nervous after having their questions answered, the doctor may advise an oral pre-med in conjunction with NuCalm™. The patient must understand that if they choose that option, they will need to have a ride to and from the clinic. With NuCalm™ alone, they will not need a ride.

NuCalm™ should be administered in the first few minutes of the patient's arrival into the clinic. After confirming the procedure with the patient and ensuring all documents and the EMR are okay, surgical staff needs to follow the steps on how to administer NuCalm™.

Once the patient has all NuCalm™ steps in place, surgical staff can place the topical anesthetic and let the doctor know the patient is ready for local anesthesia.

*The author is an investor in NuCalm™.

Appendix B

American HealthCare Lending™

American HealthCare Lending™ is a network of over 700 lenders nationwide that provide more options for patient financing at affordable rates and terms.

For the dental practice, the process is simple. Simply sign a services agreement, schedule a brief over-the-phone training, begin submitting patient applications online or via fax, and start seeing results!

With over 700 lenders in the network, more patients get approved for the financing they want with more options for better rates and terms.

Put American HealthCare Lending™ to work for you!

Contact them today at info@americanhcl.com or call toll-free 888.602.6066.

CPSIA information can be obtained at www.ICGtesting.com
Printed in the USA
LVOW05s1254230214

374828LV00017B/854/P